AIR FORCE ONE

★ THE FINAL MISSION ★

Photo by Glenn Grossman

THE
DONNING COMPANY
PUBLISHERS

AIR FORCE ONE

⭐ THE FINAL MISSION ⭐

by
Joel Haskel Cohen and Michael Steven Cohen
with Michael Broggie

The Donning Company Publishers
184 Business Park Drive, Suite 206
Virginia Beach, VA 23462

Barbara Buchanan, Office Manager
Pamela Koch, Editor
Scott Rule, Director of Marketing, Graphic Designer
Amy Thomann, Imaging Artist
Stephanie Linneman, Marketing Coordinator

Library of Congress Cataloging-in-Publication Data
Cohen, Joel Haskel, 1934-
  Air Force One : the final mission / by Joel Haskel Cohen & Michael
Steven Cohen with Michael Broggie.
     p. cm.
  Includes index.
  ISBN-13: 978-1-57864-362-2 (hard cover : alk. paper)
  ISBN-10: 1-57864-362-7 (hard cover : alk. paper)
  ISBN-13: 978-1-57864-363-9 (soft cover : alk. paper)
  ISBN-10: 1-57864-363-5 (soft cover : alk. paper)
  1. Air Force One (Presidential aircraft) 2. Ronald Reagan
Presidential Library. 3. Airplanes--Conservation and restoration-
-United States. 4. Boeing 707 (Jet transports) 5. Presidents--
Transportation--United States. 6. Antique and classic aircraft--
United States. I. Cohen, Michael Steven, 1960- II. Broggie, Michael,
1942- III. Title.
  TL723.C64 2006
  629.133'349--dc22

                        2006014506

Printed in the United States of America
at Walsworth Publishing Company, Marceline, Missouri

For more information or to order additional copies, visit:
www.AIRFORCEONETHEFINALMISSION.com.

We dedicate this book to our family for their patience and endless support.

Left to right: Larry, Rio, Joseph, Joan, Bronwyn, Elizabeth

TABLE OF CONTENTS

A SPECIAL MESSAGE FROM NANCY REAGAN

Air Force One holds so many fond memories for me. Ronnie and I spent countless wonderful hours aboard this special airplane traveling to cities and towns across the country, as well as foreign lands around the globe. I remember each journey as if it was yesterday.

I will never forget our first flight aboard Air Force One. It was just days before Ronnie's first inauguration, and President Carter generously sent the airplane to bring us from California to Washington, D.C. It was such a thrill to step aboard this majestic aircraft with "USAF" on the side and the number 27000 on her tail. It was less than a five-hour ride, but Air Force One carried us into eight years that changed our lives.

In a sense, we "lived" on Air Force One every time we flew her. We came to know the military crew who served aboard as if they were members of our own family. They took great care to plan special menus, and they treated everyone who accompanied us with the same love and respect. This unique group of people was extremely dedicated and attentive, and we were so grateful for their commitment. We knew we were in a safe and warm environment, and we always felt at home.

It even became a tradition to serve one of Ronnie's favorites—chocolate cake—if a crewmember or passenger was celebrating a milestone while aboard. I'll never forget the day that one of the Secret Service agents had a birthday. He was a rather burly fellow and took to the task of blowing out the candles with gusto. Unfortunately, Ronnie was standing directly in the line of fire (chocolate), which splattered all over his clean white shirt. Everyone laughed, including my husband, but we never hesitated to celebrate a happy occasion with chocolate cake again.

During our time at the White House, we had one extraordinary experience after another—not all of them joyful—but we knew each and every day how lucky we were to be there. Ronnie always said that Air Force One represented the spirit and democracy of the United States of America in a very unique way. It is the only symbol of our great country that could be taken "on the road," so to speak. Whenever and wherever that airplane touched down, everyone who saw it knew it represented freedom, and it carried aboard the promise of a better future.

I hope Ronnie will be remembered for many achievements, but one of his greatest objectives as President was to bring democracy to those who lived behind the Iron Curtain. I was never so proud as when Ronnie first met the leader of the Soviet Union in a one-on-one meeting in Geneva, or when he stood at the Brandenburg Gate in West Berlin and demanded an end to the Cold War, or when we traveled to Moscow where Ronnie spoke openly to students at Moscow State University. Air Force One took us to all of these places, and so many more.

Ronnie really wanted to share his experiences aboard this aircraft with everyone who never got the chance to step on board. Knowing that 27000 would be retired one day (to be replaced by a Boeing 747), my husband asked if it would be possible to bring this airplane to the Reagan Library in Simi Valley, California. I promised him we would do everything we could to make this dream a reality.

I am so proud that we have been able to fulfill Ronnie's wish. Although he could not be present when 27000 arrived in California on her last flight on September 8, 2001, I was honored to meet the airplane on his behalf. And when we dedicated the Air Force One Pavilion on October 21, 2005, I know that Ronnie was looking down upon us with his telltale grin and sense of satisfaction that she has one more mission—to tell the story of how a United States President can change the world through travel.

I am so thrilled that this aircraft has been given a permanent place of honor at the Reagan Library. I hope you will enjoy your experience onboard and share in her *Final Mission*.

Nancy Reagan

UNITED STATES OF A

This is the story of Air Force One that was almost not told. When we became aware that this historic event was going to take place and that no one had intended to document the journey, we were somehow drawn, even driven to inquire further. This was not to be a story of an aircraft's last flight, but the beginning of its final mission.

Our experience in the entertainment industry taught us how to frame a shot, how to light a scene, and how to conduct an interview, but did we have a story that people would want to see or read about? We believed the answer was "yes," but the real decision to take this journey came from something other than experience. With no TV network distribution deal in place, no crew put together, no budget, and with one of us running a hectic distribution and import business and the other truly enjoying his time on the golf course, we just looked at each other and somehow knew, this had to be done, and WE were the ones to do it.

So with the help of many, and in spite of a few, and unaware of what we were about to witness, we set about OUR mission: to capture for posterity the faces and the images of the people who became part of this project, to send one of the most important airplanes in American history off on her *Final Mission*.

While this was originally intended to be a documentary project in which we were to be the proverbial "flies on the wall," it became much more. It became personal. As with most of those involved in this project,

Michael Col

it opened our minds and hearts and enabled us to understand the majesty of history to which 27000 was a central image. As Air Force One, she represented the United States of America and all that it stands for. She was a player, and the world was her stage. And she is still a star.

As most projects progress, they tend to take on a life of their own; this one seemed to be guided by Air Force One herself. She seemed to want to get to know all those involved before she really let anything happen. Once comfortable, she let everyone shine.

There is an aura about this plane. A spirit. There's something mystical about being onboard alone with the hatch closed, when everything is quiet. There's a tranquil sense of security as though the plane is your protector. We found she has a personality—caring and light-hearted, but always demanding respect. And the walls…they do talk.

While we were not there to record the history made aboard this plane, we were privileged to witness and record a segment of history made by this plane. Detail and discovery marked our journey as documentary producers and authors of this book. We became the eyes and ears of those less fortunate, those who weren't privileged to witness this slice of American history. Now complete, it will be shared by generations who will come and marvel at this beautiful aircraft and its wonderful surroundings. It's been a grand experience—one that likely will dominate our memories for the rest of our lives.

Joel and Michael Cohen
Westlake Village, California

SPECIAL THANKS TO

Nancy Reagan
Duke Blackwood
Joanne Drake
Cary Garman
Kirby Hanson

Who understood our vision and helped us realize this project.

THANK YOU TO

(Alphabetical order)

Don Blue
The Boeing Crew
John Bouza
Steve Branch
Michael Broggie
Sharon Broggie
Marina Burgos
President George H. W. Bush
President George W. Bush
Kevin Byrne
Pat and Janet Caffrey
President Jimmy Carter
Steve Chealander
Penny Chua
President Bill Clinton
The Coast Movers Crew
Scott Conley
Roger Cosgrove
Matt Cowles
Mort Dana
Bob David
Joe DiGennaro
President Gerald Ford

Frank Gonzales
Glenn Grossman
Stan Hainer
Jim Hearn
Randy Huizenga
Joe Irvine
Pamela Koch
La Quinta Hotels
Rod Mack
Chris Mallari
Mark Milleron
Steve Mull
Greg Pineda and All Media Services
Cliff Richards
Scott Rule
The Security Staff at the Reagan Library
Brian Simons
Doug Sloniker
The Staff at the Ronald Reagan Library
Dwight Tompkins
David Ureno
Bob York

Whose contributions added to the richness of this publication.

All photographs by Michael and Joel Cohen except those individually credited.
Photographs on Presidential Retrospectives provided by respective Presidential Libraries.

WELCOME HOME

The impression most experience when seeing Air Force One for the first time is the magnificence of this airship regally perched on three points and canted slightly at two degrees toward the sky.

She appears to be in flight—like a giant eagle with wings spread—poised to leap through the huge wall of glass and soar over the rolling hills of Simi Valley toward the beckoning horizon. Standing above or viewed from below, the plane conveys a mystical spirit.

Immediately, senses attempt to compute the visual information, but the mind is challenged to comprehend reality. What finally

registers is the magnitude of the craft and the fact that she was a significant participant in global history for the past three decades.

Considered one of the most perfectly proportioned aircraft ever built, this Boeing 707-320B is representative of why America became the greatest country in

the world. The combined skills of the artist, sculptor, planner, designer, engineer, assembly crew, and, ultimately, the flight personnel are reflected in her presence comparable to a huge work of art. It's a monument to those who created her, who crewed on her, and to a country served by her.

Unique in all of aviation is the designation given to aircraft that carry the most powerful individual in the world, the President of the United States of America. The identification Air Force One is used only when the sitting President is onboard the aircraft. Otherwise, the plane is known by its tail number, in this case SAM (Special Air Mission) 27000.

This is the last Boeing 707 to see Presidential service and one that accumulated an impressive record of twenty-eight years, flying seven presidents on 445 missions, 1,440 sorties, covering 1,314,596 miles of air travel. Nearly half—211 domestic and international missions—were with President Reagan, who flew aboard 27000 more than any other President. In all, there were fifty international missions visiting more than two hundred cities worldwide during Reagan's eight years in the White House.

But this is more than a chronicle about an aircraft and its distinguished flying record, as impressive as it may be. This is also the story of how one commission ended for Air Force One and of her reassignment to a new and equally important *Final Mission*.

For generations of visitors to experience and appreciate, Air Force One is the towering centerpiece of a prestigious display in the Air Force One Pavilion at the Ronald Reagan Presidential Library and Museum in Simi Valley, California. Visitors throughout the world have the opportunity to encounter the virtually spiritual ambiance of the interior of this plane as it was June 12, 1987, on her

historic mission to Berlin, in which Reagan's declaration regarding the Berlin Wall heralded the end to the Cold War.

Open for the very first time to public tours, Air Force One represents an entire fleet that served as Presidential aircraft dating back to the administration of FDR and his "Sacred Cow," as depicted in the Pavilion's 12-feet-by-120-feet mural of aviation history created by noted artist Stan Stokes. She also represents the many military personnel who serve this nation as flight crew, maintenance, ground crew, air traffic control, and in myriad other functions, each carrying tremendous responsibility requiring the highest standard of performance. The Air Force One Pavilion celebrates the dedicated service of these people and their transportation equipment, which are used to transport the leader of the free world safely in the air and on the ground.

After construction at the Boeing factory in Renton, Washington, on July 10, 1972, the plane made her maiden flight on July 31, 1972. The Air Force accepted delivery on August 4, 1972, joining other Presidential aircraft operating from the Eighty-ninth Military Airlift Wing at Andrews Air Force Base in Maryland. Commencing her tour of duty as Air Force One on February 9, 1973, she flew President Nixon from Andrews AFB to Miramar Naval Air Station near Nixon's Western White House at San Clemente, California.

Her last flight with President Nixon aboard marked a historic first. Facing certain impeachment because of the Watergate scandal and subsequent cover-up, Nixon agreed to resign. On August 8, 1974, he and his wife, Pat, left the White House aboard Marine One helicopter for the short flight to Andrews Air Force Base where they boarded Air Force One. At noon eastern time, Gerald R. Ford was sworn in as President. The orderly transition of the Presidency had passed from Nixon to Ford, requiring the call sign of the plane to change. Precisely the same moment somewhere over Missouri on its way to California, the pilot, Colonel Ralph Albertazzie, radioed Kansas City Air Traffic Control to report that Air Force One was now SAM 27000.

Her last mission as Air Force One was August 29, 2001, for President George W. Bush, who made a short round trip flight from Waco to San Antonio, Texas. His name joined the list of six other presidents who had flown aboard the plane designated "The Spirit of American Democracy." During twenty-eight years of perfect on-time service, she carried more presidents, to more countries, for more meetings, and on more missions, than any other aircraft in history. All without a single piece of lost luggage!

Upon seeing this inspiring aircraft, one can practically feel her pride of accomplishment as the Pavilion's lighting reflects in her gleaming polished aluminum and beautiful Air Force One livery designed by renowned industrial designer Raymond Loewy. Cliff Richards of Flightline Services painstakingly restored the exterior to the original palette selected by Jacqueline Kennedy of white, silver, gold, and several shades of blue.

As visitors climb aboard through the forward hatch, they begin absorbing the detail of her internal workings seen in the flight deck, the global communications center, and the President's office and conference area. Beyond is seating for guests, staff, and press corps and the twenty-four-hour galley. Capable of flying nonstop over six thousand miles, Air Force One was an airborne White House with worldwide strategic command capabilities.

While onboard the plane, one can feel the aura of being in the presence of history. Pausing to listen quietly, voices from the past can be heard through our minds and imaginations and are captured in our hearts. In this hallowed craft, one's soul may open and be touched across the veil of time.

Rising to the challenge of preserving this craft for future generations and creating an appropriate showcase of transportation is the Ronald Reagan Presidential Foundation. With a skilled architect and a cadre of engineers, technicians, designers, and specialists representing an array of talents, this team accomplished the seemingly impossible task of dismantling, moving, reassembling, and mounting Air Force One in her new home.

Complementing the Boeing 707 is a collection of transport and support equipment used to move the President and his entourage safely from point to point. There's a Marine One helicopter, an F-14 Tomcat fighter jet, and Reagan's armored Cadillac limousine guarded by an LAPD squad car and two police motorcycles and a Secret Service SUV.

With cooperation from the United States Air Force, various governmental agencies and officials, and generous financial support from corporations and individuals, Air Force One has acquired a permanent home in a majestic pavilion on a hill. She has inaugurated her Final Mission, which will preserve for posterity a significant era of global history as a symbol of America's freedom and democracy.

As President Reagan said, *"God has given us the ability to make something from nothing. . . . The human mind is free to dream, create and perfect. Technology, plus freedom, equals opportunity and progress."*

Welcome home, Air Force One.

PRESIDENTIAL RETROSPECTIVES

THE GIFT

For an individual who candidly preferred the feel of a tooled leather saddle aboard a horse to a high-backed chair aboard Air Force One, Ronald Reagan did a lot of flying.

In fact, the fortieth President did more flying aboard Air Force One to more countries than any other President in history. That he personally didn't relish flight was not a deterrent to his global mobility. He believed it was his responsibility to travel to meetings where, as the Great Communicator, he was most effective one-on-one with his counterpart.

To get there, he had at his command the finest-equipped aircraft in the air. Air Force One had safety and security equipment well beyond that of a commercial jetliner. It bristled with communications gear linked to a network of satellites providing instantaneous contact anywhere on the ground, in the air, or at sea.

The layout of the interior cabin provided a highly efficient working environment. From the control cabin or flight deck to

the staff area and galley, every square inch was carefully planned by White House staff and Boeing design engineers to optimize the available space. Created during the administration of Dwight Eisenhower, Boeing 707s were selected for duty as Air Force One because of their reliability, endurance, and range. They were also fast. In a factory demonstration flight from Seattle to Baltimore in March 1957, a 707 covered the distance in three hours forty-eight minutes averaging 612 miles an hour. The successor aircraft was the 707-320B, designated by the Air Force as VC-137C; with a 23,000-gallon fuel capacity and four Pratt & Whitney JT3D turbofan engines, providing a range of 7,140 miles. For more than thirty years, the 707 was the prime air transport for the President.

During Reagan's White House administration, it became increasingly apparent that the President needed a larger aircraft. While the interior of the 707 was custom designed for Presidential use, its capacity was limited to fifty passengers and a crew of eighteen. The commercial model of the 707 accommodated up to 189 passengers.

Two 747s were ordered by the Air Force from Boeing with interiors designed from input provided by members of the Reagan White House staff that had flown nearly thirteen hundred hours aboard the craft.

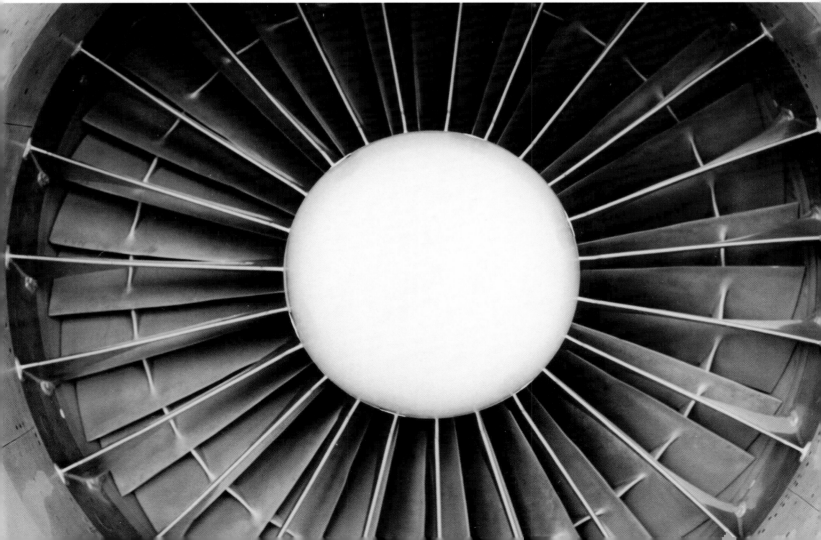

Among the added features on the new Boeing 747 were a bedroom and a bathroom with a shower for the President so he could arrive rested for his meetings. Sleep was all but impossible aboard the 707. President Reagan loved playing a practical joke on members of his cabinet and staff by being photographed standing over dozing staff members, whose pictures were likely to be posted on a White House bulletin board. The President also would sign copies of the pictures and forward them to his "victims." These lighthearted photographs are now highly valued collectibles.

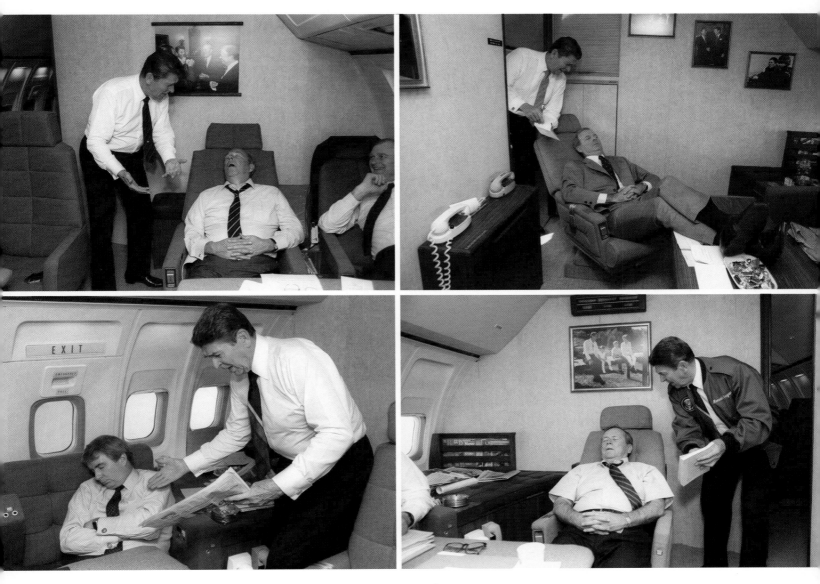

As a result of President Reagan's foresight, two 747-200s joined the fleet in 1990. For another decade, 27000 was used for flights to airports that couldn't accommodate a 747 jumbo jet and for transporting the vice president, governmental officials, and members of their families. Because delivery came after Reagan left the White House, he never flew aboard the 747 as President. However, the plane was instrumental in the conduct of his funeral, which began with a California-to-Washington flight and a return trip for interment at the Reagan Presidential Library. Many witnesses remember the slow turn the majestic 747 took over the Library upon its final approach to Point Mugu Naval Air Station.

Before leaving the White House, Reagan asked Secretary of the Air Force James F. McGovern *(right)* for a favor. When 27000 was to be retired from service, he wanted to borrow the plane to share her with the American public by creating a display at his planned Presidential library in California.

The secretary agreed to the loan but let him know that it might be a while since the plane had plenty of air miles left in her. It took about twelve years. Finally, A. L. Roche, Secretary of the Air Force, called the Reagan Foundation.

"The Air Force is retiring 27000. Do you have a place for her?"

"Absolutely!" was the excited response.

Thus, a series of events was set in motion to provide an appropriate home for Air Force One, President Reagan's longtime partner in international diplomacy. She had served him and six other presidents well during nearly three decades, so it seemed justified that such dedicated service be rewarded with a perpetual place of honor. Reagan wanted to share this gift with the American people by giving them the unique opportunity to come aboard Air Force One like a member of the White House staff or the press corps.

TOUCH DOWN

Among the military crew of Air Force One, there is a cardinal rule: Always take off and land on time.

This isn't the same standard by which commercial airlines operate. They consider anything within fifteen minutes to be "on time." When Air Force One is scheduled to take off and land, it is EXACTLY on the appointed time to the nearest second. There are no exceptions or excuses. This is one aircraft operation upon which you can set your watch. President Reagan made it a habit to congratulate his pilot, Colonel Bob Ruddick, on his punctuality every time Air Force One landed.

After an agreement and necessary clearances were secured, and it was definite that 27000 would be loaned by the Air Force to

the Reagan Presidential Library on a permanent basis, a delivery schedule was developed with the Reagan Foundation. The aircraft had been scheduled to undergo its mandatory inspection and recertification the second week of September 2001. By transferring custody and delivering the plane to the Reagan Foundation before this deadline, the Air Force could save $150,000 in certification expenses.

The one caveat was that the plane would never fly again once the Reagan Foundation took possession. This was not an issue since the plane was destined to be displayed inside a building—a building

that would enclose the aircraft so not only would it be earthbound, it wouldn't even be able to move once the final wall was completed.

Dubbed Operation Homeward Bound, September 8, 2001, was the date 27000 was to depart Andrews Air Force Base in Maryland and fly to where she would touch down for the last time at San Bernardino International Airport in California, the converted military airfield formerly known as Norton Air Force Base.

A gala reception was quickly arranged with Mrs. Ronald Reagan leading a host of dignitaries, some of whom were accorded the honor of flying aboard 27000 on her final flight. These

The Final Flight
SAM 27000
8 September 2001

Diagram labels (top to bottom): CONTROL CABIN · FORWARD ENTRY/COMMUNICATION STATION · STATE ROOM 1 · STATE ROOM 2 · LOUNGE · STAFF AREA · PASSENGER COMPARTMENT 1 · PASSENGER COMPARTMENT 2 · PASSENGER COMPARTMENT 3 · AFT ENTRY AREA

Seat	Passengers	
1	Mrs. Diane Roche	Wife of Dr. Roche
2	Ms. Heather Roche	Daugther
3	NOT CERTIFIED	
4	NOT CERTIFIED	
5	NOT CERTIFIED	
6	NOT CERTIFIED	
7	NOT CERTIFIED	
8	NOT CERTIFIED	
9	Dr. James G. Roche	Secretary of the Air Force
10	Congressman Issa	US House of Representatives
11	Mrs. Issa	Congressman's Wife
12	Congressman Calvert	US House of Representatives
13	Ms. Christine Kennedy	Professional Staff Member, House Transportation Committee
14	Michael Montelongo	SAF/FM
15	OPEN	
16	Brig Gen Rosenker	Dep. Assist. to the President and Dir., White House Military Office
17	Hector F. Irastorza, Jr.	Dep. Assist. to the President for Management and Admin.
18	Brad Blakeman	Dep. Assist. to the President and Director of Scheduling
19	Joanne Drake	Chief of Staff, Office of Ronald Reagan
20	Fredrick Ryan	Chairman of the Board, Reagan Presidential Foundation
21	Mark Burson	Executive Director, Reagan Presidential Foundation
22	Duke Blackwood	Director, Ronald Reagan Presidential Library
23	Hugh Sidney	Correspondent
24	USAF STENO	
25	Maj Gen Leroy Barnidge	SAF/LL
26	Lt Gen Lance Lord	AF/CVA
27	Brig Gen (S) Glenn Spears	89th Airlift Wing Commander
28	Col Mark Tillman	The Presidential Pilot
29	Maj Law	
30	Maj Richard M. Murphy	Aide
31	Lt Col Lee Cox	Executive officer to Gen Lord
32	Maj William "Sweet" Tart	SAF/LL, Assist. to Gen Barnidge
33	SMSgt Greg A. Enwright	Personal Security officer
34	Long	
35	Alma Brown	
36	Maj Chester Curtis	Public Affairs officer
37	Brian Hopkins	Photographer
38	William "Joe" Chappell	Former AFO Flight Engineer
39	John Haigh	Former AFO Flight Attendant
40	James Jackson	Former AFO Navigator
41	Steven Hammel	Vice Presidents, US News
42	Robert Brown	Former AFO Chief/Maintenance
43	Willie Falcon	Former AFO Chief/Maintenance
44	OPEN	
45	Howard Franklin	Former AFO Flight Attendant
46	Charles Palmer	Former AFO Flight Attendant
47	Richard Holley	Former AFO Communications NCO
48	Lee Simmons	Former AFO Flight Attendant
49	Stump	
50	Linda Franklin	Former AFO Information Manager
51	Doerr	
52	Varhegy	
53	USAF Security	
54	USAF Security	
55	Firmin	
56	Byron	
57	OPEN	
58	OPEN	

Flight Crew

Robinson, James T.	LTC
Brunskloe, Daniel K.	LTC
Tillman, Mark W.	COL
Pavelko, George L.	LTC
Whithed, David M.	MSG
Mancuso, John A.	TSG
Tedford, Michael W.	CMS
Moren, Edwin H.	CMS
Casy, Daniel P.	MSG
Wiman, Michael D.	MSG
Williams, Randy C.	TSG
Varon, Pamela J.	SSG
Purden, Elizabeth L.	TSG
Balfour, Richard L.	SSG
Blacaflor, Allan R.C.	SSG
Monroe, Marlin D.	TSG

included government officials, members of the Reagan Foundation, representatives of the news media, and current and retired members of the Air Force One crew.

The 707, with her unmistakable markings and large black "United States of America" lettering across the fuselage, loomed into view in the hazy afternoon sky above the Inland Empire of Southern California. Instead of a direct approach and landing, pilot Lieutenant Colonel James T. Robinson performed a ceremonial flyby as the four jet engines roared five hundred feet above the crowd gathered on the tarmac. The pilot put 27000 into a steep left turn and leveled off for landing. As the gear was being lowered, a spontaneous cheer went up from the audience of invited guests. Blue smoke billowed from the eight tires on the main landing gear followed by a puff of smoke from the two tires on the nose gear—signaling that the plane had completed her final touchdown. Everyone watching became a witness to history as twenty-eight years of distinguished flying was coming to an end.

The plane rolled up and stopped exactly on point. A portable ramp was moved into place as the engines shut down for the last time. The forward hatch opened, revealing the Presidential Seal on the inside. As passengers deplaned, many stopped to savor the moment and to pose for photographs. These pictures would become family heirlooms.

This airport was selected by the Reagan Foundation because it had empty hangars with enough capacity to accommodate the Boeing 707 with a vertical stabilizer that reached 42 feet 5 inches from the ground, a wing span of 145 feet 9 inches, and a fuselage 152 feet 11 inches in length.

A key individual who became involved in Operation Homeward Bound at the outset was Don Blue, owner of Blue Aviation located at San Bernardino International Airport.

Blue had received a call from an Air Force official informing him that 27000 was coming to the airport. With an excellent reputation developed over forty years in all facets of aviation operations, the Air Force asked him to ensure responsibility for deactivating the aircraft upon its arrival to assure that it would never fly again. Blue signed an agreement with the military branch guaranteeing that he would fulfill the assignment. The document was signed the day the aircraft arrived.

Operationally, the first task following the arrival ceremony was purging the fuel from the tanks. Once this was done, the plane was towed into Hangar 795, known as the Sheriff's Hangar because the local law enforcement agency had used it to store aerial equipment.

Before anything could be touched on the aircraft, the government had one last operation to be handled by the Air Force and other federal security operatives. For the first twenty-four hours that 27000 was in the hangar, the doors were closed and secured

by armed military guards and deputies from the San Bernardino County Sheriff's Department. What was removed remains top secret, but because the plane was equipped with the latest in communications and encryption devices and a missile defense system, it's obvious that national security was necessarily given top priority. Once the black SUVs departed with their precious cargo, the plane was ready for its next phase.

To prepare 27000 for nearly eighteen months of storage, she was carefully cleaned inside and out. Prior to securing the aircraft, the weight of the plane had to be determined for the issuance of a permit from the California Department of Transportation (Caltrans) to move the aircraft on public highways. Don Blue said he tried for a week to get the information from Boeing. A Boeing official said they had no data on this aircraft; for security reasons, the files had been removed and no information was available. The Reagan Foundation contacted the California Highway Patrol, which had jurisdiction over the move. The CHP brought to the airport four large portable scales used for field inspections of trucks using California freeways. The information was communicated to Caltrans.

During this time, the Reagan Foundation board of directors moved ahead with planning for Air Force One Pavilion and hired an architectural firm and a construction company.

Meanwhile, the Foundation was challenged with the cost and operation of preparing the plane for its move to the Library. The Boeing Company, the original manufacturer of the craft, was the obvious choice to conduct the dismantling procedure. Operating numerous plants in Southern California with more than 35,000 of its 145,000 workers, Boeing is the largest employer in the state. For over sixty years, Boeing has been building aircraft used to transport United States presidents dating back to Franklin D. Roosevelt, who flew aboard a Boeing 314 Dixie Clipper seaplane in 1943 to meet secretly with Winston Churchill in Casablanca, Morocco. It was the first flight by a U.S. President.

THE HISTORY OF THE FLYING WHITE HOUSE

BY STAN STOKES

TOUCH DOWN

It wasn't until John F. Kennedy's term in the White House that Air Force One became the Secret Service code name for aircraft carrying the President. Kennedy liked the name so well that he told his staff and the White House press corps to make the reference known to the public. According to a recent survey, nearly 80 percent of adults recognize Air Force One as the President's plane.

To serve as consulting project manager of the Air Force One project, the Reagan Foundation selected Robert H. David, a native of Redondo Beach, California, with fifteen years experience as a general contractor in heavy industrial construction. He was to be responsible for overseeing the building of Air Force One Pavilion and furnishing it with its contents, including 27000 and the Marine One helicopter.

The major engineering challenge in the project was removal of the wings and stabilizers from 27000, which were specifically designed and installed so that they would never come off. An additional challenge was that the aircraft's beautiful exterior had to be preserved. When reassembled, 27000 had to look exactly as she did when serving as Air Force One.

A meeting was held at the hangar to discuss how the plane would be dismantled. Two differing opinions emerged. One was to remove the wings and stabilizers with cutting torches. Others wanted to remove them surgically by extracting each individual fastener. All agreed that the cosmetic integrity of the plane had to be preserved. To accomplish this, Don Blue recommended recruiting a crew from Boeing. He contacted a group he called the "antiquers," who

loved to restore vintage aircraft. They agreed to do the project if the Reagan Foundation covered their expenses, but the Foundation said they didn't have the budget to cover the cost. By this time, senior executives at Boeing had learned about the project from the Ronald Reagan Foundation and had agreed to consider sponsoring the project.

The Foundation contacted Rudy deLeon *(right)*, senior vice president of Boeing's Washington, D.C., operations, to seek his company's help. DeLeon embraced the idea, and after several meetings, Boeing agreed to handle the daunting task. The value of Boeing's participation was well over one million dollars plus the unique expertise of its engineers.

"By restoring and preserving President Reagan's Air Force One, we not only honor him, we are also giving all Americans a glimpse of his Presidency," said deLeon. **"This project has brought great anticipation and pride to the people at Boeing."**

BOEING

PRESIDENTIAL RETROSPECTIVES

To be very honest, I felt safe, secure, and comfortable every time I stepped onto that very special aircraft.

Everyone onboard the aircraft, from the President, the press, the staff, and the Secret Service, could relax and find rejuvenating relief from the rigors of a political campaign or the obligations of protocol while representing the United States overseas.

The crew of Air Force One was outstanding. It goes without saying that they were the finest professionals and, as far as I was concerned, my good friends who personally cared about me and every other individual traveling aboard the aircraft.

Colonel Les McClelland was the pilot during my tenure as President. I always remember him as a "gentle giant." Les played football for Syracuse and had a short career playing in the Canadian Football League. With a smile, he imparted tremendous confidence. Things may not be perfect on any given day, but once aboard that aircraft, everything was fine. Les was big and he was strong. I always felt he could handle that "big bird" without any hydraulic assistance.

We had some incidents, which were rare in their occurrence. I believe we were traveling to Finland for the Helsinki Conference when the Swedish jet fighters came up and took positions off the flanks of Air Force One. They caused more than a little excitement for all the passengers.

Air Force One—SAM 27000—was truly a home in the sky. The President and Commander-in-Chief would have around him trusted staff, very often family, good friends, a respectful press corps, and the comfort and security provided by Secret Service and the crew. With humble respect and admiration, I will tell you that airplane, that magnificent airplane, was truly the wind beneath my wings.

Gerald R. Ford

SURGICAL TEAM

Just because no one had ever taken apart a 707 bolt by bolt didn't mean it couldn't be done.

More important was accepting the responsibility for a national treasure. The management of Boeing recognized this as an opportunity to showcase one of the company's finest creations and offer a worthwhile and challenging project to its people, for which they could be justly proud.

By doing so, Boeing ultimately saved the Library $1.5 million in costs related to delivering the plane to her final destination inside Air Force One Pavilion. Even more than generous financial support, Boeing provided expert technicians and engineers. Combined with the forty-year background of Don Blue, the Operation Homeward

Bound team of talent appeared capable of handling the delicate process of dismantling and reassembling this aviation work of art.

In February 2003, Boeing assigned one of its veteran aircraft construction directors, John Bouza, to lead Operation Homeward Bound. His four-decade career in aviation was primarily with McDonnell Douglas, which merged with Boeing in August of 1997.

"We were excited about getting the airplane into its new home," commented Bouza, director of production support operations for the C-17 program at Boeing's facility in Long Beach, California. "The finished project certainly reflects the pride that the Boeing Company and its employees have toward this airplane and its significance to America's heritage."

He assigned his managing assistant, Kevin Byrne (white hat), to handle the daily details of the project, which began with selecting a crew of qualified technicians.

Among the aircraft industry's resources is a group of men who are skilled at dismantling aircraft. This is necessary when a plane is involved in a crash or lands somewhere other than at an airport. Often they are rapidly deployed to locations throughout the world to handle all manner of aircraft salvages, usually under emergency conditions. Operation Homeward Bound was to be one of the most unique assignments for this assembled crew: Rene Rodriguez, Oscar Diaz, John Nguyen, Jose Magana, Miguel Martinez, Harold Archleta, George L. Duran Jr., Bill S. Rhodes, En Sockhom, Khoa Duong, Roderick Mack, David Ureno, Juan Carlos Parra, Frank Gonzales, George L. Duran Sr., Juan Juarez, Ramon Sanchez, and Erick Mann.

First, the plane had to be moved to a larger hangar where there would be sufficient area to dismantle the wings and the vertical and horizontal stabilizers. Hangar 695 was known as the "Disney Hangar" among airport personnel because it was the site previously used by Walt Disney Imagineers to fabricate and test a new attraction called "StormRider," which they had designed for DisneySea at Tokyo Disney Resort. It was recommended that the City of San Bernardino rent the hangar to the Disney Company, which agreed to finance the then needed improvements to the hangar including electrical repairs, window replacement, repair of an overhead hoist, and restoration of the huge hangar doors on their tracks. The Disney Imagineers used the hangar for their secret work for about a year.

While Disney Imagineers specialize in creating magic, a different brand of magic was about to be performed—the removal of all major components from the fuselage of Air Force One while preserving its perfect condition.

On June 1, 2003, after eighteen months of storage, the aircraft was towed out of the Sheriff's Hangar and washed down by airport fire suppression equipment with high-pressure nozzles. It was then moved into the Disney Hangar.

To begin, the crew had to locate each fastener. These fasteners are designed to expand when inserted so that they don't work loose with friction. There are thirteen hundred fasteners on each wing. Called huck bolts, they are made of titanium and are kept on dry ice prior to being inserted in a hole that is retained by an aligning device called a "cleeco." The cleeco is removed, and the frozen huck

bolt is installed. As it warms to the ambient temperature, it expands and is practically impossible to remove. Bill Rhodes, a mechanic who has the precise moves of a surgeon, found the only way to remove the huck bolts was to drill them and fracture them into pieces much as a dentist does with a stubborn wisdom tooth.

Through years of service, numerous coats of paint had filled the heads of the fasteners so each had to be carefully located and circled with a felt tip marker pen. The first screw to be removed was from an access panel under the right wing. As Rod Mack was removing it to be numbered and bagged, he dropped the screw on the concrete floor. He rather nonchalantly inquired of those watching and filming the scene, "Did anyone see where that went?" The crew laughed nervously and then sighed with relief when someone spotted the screw and quickly retrieved it for tagging and bagging. Numerous small, white, cloth drawstring bags were used to hold the numbered parts, and the contents were entered into a computerized data bank. Each part was treated as a national treasure.

In addition to the overhead hoist, forklifts and large portable cranes were brought in to stabilize the components as they were detached. The wings each weighed 18,400 pounds and were nearly seventy-five feet long and thirty-five feet wide.

The first step was removing the four Pratt & Whitney engines weighing seven thousand pounds each. Since the engines were designed for easy removal to facilitate routine maintenance, this step went rather quickly. They were placed in cradles and moved out of the way.

The task would become much tougher.

Next was removing the left horizontal stabilizer. John Bouza had secured construction drawings for the 707-320B from Boeing headquarters in Renton, Washington. The crew had to figure the "pick point" on the stabilizer. Selecting the pick point of the parts was extremely important. This was the point where the weight of a wing or stabilizer was centered so the cables could be attached properly to avoid a sudden shift in the load that could have resulted in the piece crashing to the floor.

The removal procedure also required careful coordination between assistant project manager David Ureno and the crew. A clear understanding among the crew was that only one person would communicate with the hoist operator to avoid confusion.

This was critical because when the last fastener was released from the fuselage, the stabilizer would swing free, and it had to be secured. While much smaller than the wings, the horizontal stabilizers are 22 feet 8 inches long and 18 feet 11 inches wide. Each weighs two thousand pounds—about the weight of a small car.

The wings and stabilizers are made of hardened aluminum alloy that is pound-for-pound stronger than steel. Since no one had ever disassembled an aircraft in this manner, the process was a study in "engineering on the fly." Supervisor Frank Gonzales and his crew held morning and evening meetings to discuss each step. Often, a quick sketch was produced, and a needed device was welded together overnight for the next day's operation. Basic to each step

◊ SURGICAL TEAM ◊

was safety. All potential hazards were discussed, and measures were implemented to prevent injuries.

One of the most challenging tasks was handled by a diminutive member of the team named Khoa Duong. Experienced in aircraft salvage, his small frame made him the ideal candidate to crawl inside the tail section of the fuselage to access the internal fasteners for the stabilizers. Even so, the crew found that a special hydraulic impact wrench was needed to loosen the main bolts. A quick call to Boeing engineers at the company's Renton, Washington, headquarters got the tool delivered overnight.

With the agility of a gymnast, Khoa could maneuver into the smallest crawl spaces. He even limited his intake of liquid so he wouldn't have to crawl out of the fuselage to visit the restroom. When asked how long it might take to remove the fasteners, Khoa replied, "About an hour." Seven days later, he was still removing the internal fasteners for the first horizontal stabilizer even though he stayed on his task for hours at a time without a break.

Ingenuity was the operative word for finding solutions. When it became evident that the hard surfaces of the hydraulic lifts and the concrete hangar floor might damage the stabilizers, Frank Gonzales suggested getting used mattresses and spreading them out to cushion the parts. Several of the crew went to a local mattress company and obtained old, rather fragrant mattresses that had been left outside in a storage area. They proved to be perfect protectors for the delicate pieces.

As construction cost estimates grew for the Air Force One Pavilion, operating budgets tightened at the Foundation. It became imperative to relocate the plane from the airport to the Reagan Library to save the $10,000-a-month hangar rent.

The crew shifted into high gear when Air Force One project manager Bob David delivered the news that 27000 had to be moved to the Reagan Library in less than three weeks. The crew was told the move date would be June 20, 2003. The California Highway Patrol and Caltrans, which would provide the permit for the relocation, dictated this date.

Several challenges had to be met before the plane could be moved.

The sequence of removal had started with the left horizontal stabilizer, which proved to be tricky. When the last fastener was removed, the piece suddenly swung free because the estimated pick

SURGICAL TEAM

point was off center. Due to contingency planning, an additional line of cable helped to steady the piece so it didn't break loose and fall. A scissor lift with mattress padding was in place to receive the stabilizer safely. To create a safe place for the removed parts, the crew fashioned two steel jigs, lined them with several layers of old carpet obtained from a local carpet store, and used them to cradle the horizontal stabilizers.

This operation was followed by the right horizontal stabilizer, which went much smoother and faster. Next was the large vertical stabilizer, also called the tail, which carries the unique designation of 27000 and the Stars and Stripes. The vertical stabilizer was a challenge because it was fastened with large anchor screw bolts that Khoa Duong had to loosen with an impact hammer from inside.

First, the chains from the large overhead hoist were attached to bolts that had been fastened to the tail. Once one side of the base was detached, it could be lowered in the opposite direction by the hoist, as though it had a large hinge. Now horizontal, the remaining anchor screw bolts could be removed—thus releasing the entire tail section, which was laid on a pad of old mattresses.

Another issue was stabilizing the fuselage as parts came off and weight and stress points shifted from one side of the plane to the other. The left stabilizer proved to be particularly stubborn. It was as though the plane

27000

was resisting the removal of a major organ from her body. "Who are these people, and why are they operating on me?" she seemed to ask rhetorically. In time, the parts became easier to detach. The plane apparently accepted her inevitable fate and almost seemed to relax.

The wings required major team effort. They had to consider this question: What would happen to the plane when the weight of 18,400 pounds of one wing (without engines) was suddenly removed? The team came up with the solution. They designed a twenty-foot-long steel tripod with a center bolt that would stabilize the aircraft so it wouldn't rotate. It was welded overnight by Randy Huizenga, who was recommended to the project by Ken Adams of SSI, a trucking company. According to the team, Huizenga was one of the finest and quickest welders they had ever worked with. He was also a highly respected big rig driver with over twenty years experience moving heavy loads.

The tripod device was anchored to the floor and bolted to the plane. In addition, two members of the crew went to a local Home

Depot and bought numerous 2x4s, which were fashioned into a large cradle to provide additional security for the fuselage. This done, the wings could be safely removed without the risk of damage to either the wings or fuselage.

To prepare for the removal of the wings, railroad ties were stacked into "cribs" under each wing and padded with layers of used carpet. These structures would serve as resting surfaces for the wings after removal. The flap on the left wing was the first item to be addressed. Because of the extensive array of control mechanisms, hydraulic tubing, and electrical conduit necessary to operate the flaps against terrific air pressure, their removal was difficult and time consuming. Unlike other components on the plane, the flaps didn't provide much visibility into their inner workings. Just when it appeared that everything was unhooked and the flap should be free, another attachment was discovered. With perseverance, the crew finally got the flap to come free.

Coast Machinery Movers had been contracted by the Reagan Foundation to provide the cranes used in the hangar and heavy moving equipment necessary to transport the plane and her parts. Coast had a distinguished record of accomplishing seemingly impossible tasks, such as moving entire contents of plants filled with massive machinery weighing thousands of tons.

On the morning of Coast's arrival at the San Bernardino International Airport, the amount of heavy-duty equipment, including large diesel trucks hauling long flatbed trailers, mobile cranes of various sizes, and other moving equipment, took on the appearance of an Army battalion arriving at a battlefield. Somehow, members of the news media learned that this was the day that the wings would be removed. Combined with Coast's arrival, the television cameras and lighting equipment contributed to a highly dramatic scene in the hangar.

A meeting was quickly assembled with all parties to clarify the duties and responsibilities each would undertake from this point forward. In effect, Boeing handed off the physical end of the project while maintaining the critical role of guide and advisor. The mission was reviewed against the timeline imposed by the move date. It was clear that battle conditions would have to be implemented to meet the state-mandated schedule to use the freeway system. If the move weren't executed on June 20, there would be a three-week delay before another window would open in the Caltrans-and-CHP-coordinated heavy move calendar. This delay would cost the project another month's hangar rent plus the expense of the crew and all the equipment necessary for the move.

The most delicate operation of the disassembly was removal of the wings. To accomplish this, a large mobile crane and two forklift cranes were attached to the wing with cables linked to spanners. With Coast's foreman, Marcelino Palma, conducting the operation with hand signals, the three crane operators were directed to slowly and simultaneously lift the wing to a slight diagonal position to relieve pressure between the top of the wing and the body of the fuselage. Unlike engines, which are easily removed to undergo routine maintenance and major overhauls, wings are secured to planes in such a way that they should never separate from the main fuselage, for obvious reasons.

Instead of using a cutting torch that would have scarred the aircraft's pristine surface, the thirteen hundred fasteners securing each wing had to be removed individually by hand tools. It took three full days to remove the fasteners from the left wing. As Palma and the operators of the cranes began to maneuver the wing slowly away from the fuselage, it started to resist. A control cable was still attached. First spotted by Rod Mack, he grabbed a power hacksaw and, before anyone could object, inserted his arm between the fuselage and the wing and, with a quick and precise movement, severed the cable.

Fortunately, the highly skilled crane operators were applying outward pressure to the wing. After Mack performed his surgical cut on the cable, the wing swung away from the plane, and a spontaneous cheer rose from the crew. No one wanted to consider the potential consequences to Rod Mack's arm had the wing not been properly secured. The wing was then safely lowered to the makeshift three-foot-high crib supports made of railroad ties cushioned with used carpet.

Again, experience proved to be the best teacher. It took only one day to complete the removal of the right wing.

While filming the operation, a member of the documentary production crew described the ensemble of crane operators, mechanics, and crew foreman as being like ballet dancers and an orchestra, each contributing to an artistic performance of balance and precision under the direction of a conductor. At any given time, as many as twelve crewmembers were working in harmony on various parts of the plane.

New fasteners for the wings were acquired and delivered to a local precision machine shop where a fraction of the threaded surfaces were trimmed so they would be easy to install later during reassembly at the Pavilion.

That accomplished, the challenge facing the Homeward Bound Team was to find a way to move the 152-foot-11-inch-long fuselage without tweaking the frame or damaging its delicate skin.

PREPARING

Roger Cosgrove, Coast's vice president and general manager, and his sales engineer, Doug Sloniker, invited the project crew to visit their equipment yard in Fontana, California, to select what was needed for the move.

The first inclination was to place the fuselage on a long lowboy trailer. Don Blue, however, had a different thought. His concept was to utilize the structure where the landing gear was attached to the fuselage to support the plane during the move. He reasoned that this would prevent damage that could be caused by pressure from the surface of the trailer against the 65,000-pound weight of the body of the plane while traveling over the 102 miles on Southern California freeways to the Reagan Library in Simi Valley. Blue knew from his earlier experience at Boeing that the landing gear and structural supports had to withstand nine times the force of gravity. Even the earthquake-modified California freeways aren't quite that rough.

54

TO MOVE

While most of the crew was looking at a long lowboy trailer, Don Blue wandered alone among the various hauling devices until he spotted what he thought was needed: two large quad sets of wheels. One of the Coast staff members informed him that the wheels came from North American Rockwell, which used the hydraulic-powered wheel sets to move the space shuttle in its hangar while it was under construction. They pulled out their tapes and measured everything on one of the quad sets and figured, in their mind's eye, how it would work.

That night, plans were drawn up for how the wheels could be attached to a massive piece of aluminum that was the rear support for the wing, which carried through the center section of the fuselage. Since this was the strongest area of the plane, the crew reasoned they could drill holes and bolt steel plates to each side of this structure. To the plates, they could attach steel beams. Additional plates and beams would attach to where the leading edges of the wings had been located. The crew also figured they would have the margin needed for clearance in case the hydraulic pressure in the quad wheel sets failed. The next morning, after reviewing the plans, everyone agreed to the concept, and the crew went to work installing the unorthodox rigging device to the wells from where the main wings and landing gear struts had been removed.

Once the steel plates were bolted to the aluminum structure, the beam was tack welded and then taken to an offsite shop where it was strength welded to handle the weight of the fuselage. This was how the crew did things: start with a clean sheet of paper; do a quick concept sketch; and then add a piece of metal at a time until the solution was achieved with an acceptable margin of safety.

After the welding shop did its quick job, the beams were installed and the quad wheel sets were bolted to the structure. The quads rested on six-by-six-inch wooden beams laid across heavy-duty jack tables. Two large cranes were positioned to hoist the fuselage with heavy bands of webbing. While the fuselage was suspended, all the attachments that the crew had installed were carefully inspected. Once everyone was satisfied, the backup safety equipment and cradles were removed, and the plane was slowly lowered to the floor of the hangar onto its improvised running gear—the very last "flight" of 27000.

Towing presented another opportunity to exercise ingenuity. At first, it was assumed the plane could be towed by its front landing gear, as airport ground crews operating mechanical "mules" move commercial aircraft. Then it was realized that the nose gear would make the plane too high to clear the lowest overpass, so it had to be replaced with something else.

First, the nose gear was removed. A replacement structure was designed to bolt to the original connecting points. To make the height adjustable, a hydraulic ram was added. The rigging consisted of a wide axle attached at the center to the structure that had been fitted up into the landing gear well. With the wide axle, a tight turning radius could be achieved without hitting the fuselage with the wheels. To this device, the crew hooked a custom-built tow bar that had a sliding collar on a shaft, forming an A-frame to the axle. Along with the main quad units, the plane had the necessary equipment to become a surface vehicle. The crane operators carefully lowered the heavy fuselage onto its new wheels. After a careful inspection, everything appeared to be ready for testing.

A Peterbilt tractor was brought in from SSI Trucking Company, a subcontractor to Coast Machinery Movers. It had a nineteen-thousand-pound concrete counterweight installed over the drive wheels to provide traction for the high torque 600-horsepower engine. The tractor was coupled to the tow bar at its pintle hitch rather than on the fifth wheel disk.

After confirming with Air Traffic Control that San Bernardino International Airport was closed to all arrivals and departures, Randy Huizenga fired the supercharged engine to life, belching diesel smoke from its twin chrome stacks. Slowly, he hauled the fuselage out of the hangar and about a hundred yards across the tarmac. Huizenga then stopped so the crew could adjust the alignment of the wheels to prevent the plane from "doglegging." He then hauled it about a quarter of a mile on the main landing strip and stopped again so the crew could refine the adjustments. Running on the strip was helpful because the smooth concrete revealed the slightest misalignment in the rigging. After turning circles to check the clearance of the front wheels, and after several refined adjustments, the alignment was corrected from twenty-four inches to within one inch.

Back at the hangar, several lowboy trailers arrived to make the initial transfer of parts to the Library. This included two large cargo containers filled with miscellaneous equipment from the plane. Four engines were also loaded on the trailers along with the two main landing gear assemblies. The engines were fitted with blue intake covers printed with the distinctive red "Fox Face" logo of the Eighty-ninth Airlift Wing.

The convoy of trucks, including two loaded with the horizontal and vertical stabilizers, was dispatched on June 19, 2003, to the Reagan Library where the parts and cargo containers were offloaded and stored in a fenced area of the visitors' parking lot. They would languish there for eighteen months before their reunion with the fuselage. This initial move of Air Force One's components was accomplished without incident, instilling Reagan Foundation's management and the crew at the hangar with the confidence that they would complete Operation Homeward Bound without any major mishaps. However, there were still about 137 feet of wings and sixty thousand pounds of fuselage yet to be transferred.

After the crew was satisfied with its road-worthiness, the fuselage was returned to the hangar to prepare it for the main event. In the waning hours, much yet needed to be done to chart and navigate the route by the support companies in conjunction with the California Highway Patrol and Caltrans. With the countdown inexorably continuing, the project was taking on the appearance of a paramilitary maneuver.

The crew wasn't completely satisfied with how the tow bar rigging was operating. They wanted the collar to slide more smoothly along the bar. While using a handheld grinder to shape the steel piece, Blue's shirt got caught in the wheel and wrapped the material

⊛ PREPARING TO MOVE ⊛

around his hand so he couldn't let go of the trigger. The shirt caused the grinder to be pulled into his stomach. A quick-thinking member of the documentary crew filming the scene grabbed the power cord and yanked it free of its electrical socket. Not unlike John Wayne in one of his bravado war movies, Blue waved off suggestions to get his wound treated and returned to grinding until he finished the job.

Very early the next morning, a paramedic who reported to the hangar to accompany the run to the Reagan Library spotted the torn shirt and asked, "What happened to you?" That was when he finally got his wound dressed. Fortunately, it was shallow and didn't require stitches.

For the amount of time available to solve all the details, the rigging was quite ingenious. Most of all, it had to be a fail-safe system. As with the on-time delivery of the President to his destination, there was no acceptable excuse for error.

PRESIDENTIAL RETROSPECTIVES

My two most memorable trips in Air Force One were actually when I was not President of the United States. The first was in January 1977, when my family, close friends, and I embarked at Albany, Georgia, and were flown to Washington for my inauguration. It is difficult to imagine what a thrill this was.

The other unforgettable flight in 27000 came four years later, the day after I returned from the White House to my home in Plains. Along with a small group of cabinet officers and White House staff members, I was flown to Wiesbaden, Germany, to welcome the hostages who had been held in captivity by Iranian militants.

I had spent the last three days and nights of my administration conducting the extremely complex negotiations that led to their release. These brave men and women were sitting in an airplane at the end of the Tehran airport at 10:00 a.m. on inauguration day, and they had taken off for freedom a few minutes after I had relinquished the reins of government.

To embrace each one of them, with many tears, was one of the high points of my life. On the way home, we had a grand celebration!

Jimmy Carter

ALL SYSTE

With the coordinated efforts of the California Highway Patrol, California Department of Transportation, and the companies hired by the Reagan Foundation, the short deadline to plan the move of Air Force One to the Reagan Library progressed without delay.

One of the services provided by the CHP and Caltrans was up-to-the-minute status reports on road conditions throughout the state. They maintain computer records of closures for repairs and construction of roads, bridges, and barriers. This information is essential to operators such as the Permit Company of Monterey Park, California, which received the assignment from Coast Machinery Movers to survey and navigate the route from San

Bernardino International Airport to the Reagan Library. For example, Chris Mollno and his company's technicians discovered the lowest clearance along the entire route was the Cochran Street Bridge, which crosses over the 118 Ronald Reagan Freeway in Simi Valley, a few miles before the exit to the Library. With the use of a boom mounted on a pickup truck, they electronically measured each overhang that posed a potential threat along the route. They also surveyed the radii of entrances and exits that might be used along the freeway system in the event of an emergency.

With road condition data and recommendations from the CHP and Caltrans, approval was granted to Coast to make the move. As word about the move of Air Force One spread among CHP officers, there was considerable interest in volunteering for the escort detail. In actuality, the operation would be quite similar to the rolling "block and clear" procedure used to control freeway traffic and to provide security for the President. In this case, the transport of a 707 airliner over Southern California's freeways was much more intriguing than a Presidential entourage. A total of sixteen patrol units were assigned to handle the dual runs of wings and fuselage, which was scheduled to commence at midnight, June 20, 2003.

To test for clearances of the large wings, the Permit Company recommended that a skeleton of a wing be constructed and loaded onto a flatbed trailer. A quick trip to a local Home Depot store produced enough PVC pipe and twine to approximate the wing. When the trial run was made, it revealed that the numerous street lamps located on mile-long Presidential Drive leading from Madera Avenue to the Library would have to be removed. At the head of the

drive leading onto the grounds of the Library, a landscaped circular island would have to be traversed, and a large wooden gate and a security camera pole would require temporary removal. When the Library was built in 1991, no one thought to engineer the access road to accommodate a 707.

As each impeding barrier was identified and the information radioed to Coast's field management, a crew was activated to eliminate it. To handle removing the street lamps, a call went to Joe Irvine, superintendent of the project for Hathaway Dinwiddie, the construction company building the Pavilion. They provided electricians and laborers to unbolt the poles from their concrete bases, allowing a crane operator to lower the lamps to the ground.

Meanwhile, at the San Bernardino International Airport, the wings were loaded onto two long trailers. It was determined that the main gate wasn't wide enough to permit the wings to exit the airfield. A more direct route was north toward Third Street, but there wasn't any gate at that location. To solve this problem, a fence company removed enough of the chain link fencing to create a large temporary exit gate.

69

Discussion ensued about the esthetics of the fuselage. Joe DiGennaro, director of photography on the documentary film crew, recommended that the nose cone be reattached to make the plane more photogenic. It had been removed so radar equipment and other classified instruments could be dismantled. A representative of the Reagan Foundation agreed, and the nose cone was installed. The film crew director also suggested that lighting fixtures be placed along the fuselage to provide visibility of the plane. The crew quickly affixed florescent fixtures to the sides of the plane and wired them to a generator attached to the bracing of one of the quad wheel assemblies.

The CHP called an all-hands meeting in the hangar with Caltrans, Coast Machinery Movers, the Permit Company, Boeing, the documentary production crew, Reagan Foundation representatives, the mobile tire repair technician, and the paramedics. With all agreeing they were ready, the launch sequence was activated. Each participant checked radio frequencies and cell phone battery levels. Ray Blackwell, the CHP commanding officer, briefed the drivers of the rigs and camera vans. He described the procedures his officers would execute to control traffic and to keep the curious from getting too close. Members of the team were given specific instructions according to their role and responsibility.

The weather forecast predicted a thick cloud deck with a chance of light drizzle near the San Gabriel Mountains. For safety reasons, the use of a helicopter with an aerial camera aboard was cancelled.

An impromptu celebration ensued as wives, families, and friends showed up to watch the launch. With many waving small American flags, it took on the atmosphere of a military sendoff to a foreign battlefield. At 11:00 p.m., with the lights at the airport turned on and the colored lights flashing atop the vehicles, the wings left for the Library through the new gate in the north fence led by a pilot truck and a camera van and shepherded by eight CHP units.

Two hours later, at 1:00 a.m., Randy Huizenga climbed into the cab of the large Peterbilt tractor. On the seat he found a gift. It was a teddy bear with a note attached. The hand-lettered note said, "Happy Father's Day. I love you Dad." It was signed "Jacob," his four-year-old son. Huizenga paused for a moment holding the bear in hands that were made strong by years of welding and big rig driving. He reflected on the fact that the incredibly long hours on this project had kept him from spending any time with his youngest son. At that point, Bob David, the project's manager, climbed into the passenger seat and gave the "go" command. He would serve as co-pilot for the run to the Reagan Library.

Huizenga depressed the clutch and engaged the twenty-eight-gear transmission, and the cobbled rig began moving toward the exit onto Third Street. Traveling east, the plan was to make a ninety-degree right-angled turn at the intersection of Third and Alabama Avenue rather than use a diagonal shortcut that had a yield sign posted where it joined Alabama. Yet, Huizenga opted to take the diagonal route, but the fuselage was too long to clear the yield sign. Huizenga hit his air brakes before contact was made between the sign and the fuselage. Immediately recognizing the situation, several men grabbed the steel signpost and attempted to work it free of its concrete foundation by pushing it back and forth.

After several minutes, it became clear that the signpost wasn't going to give. A sledgehammer was tried with similar results. Finally, several of the larger fellows on the crew got on one side and pushed the sign until it was nearly horizontal to the ground. This late-night drama unfolded with CHP officers watching with curiosity as public property was being compromised. A couple of crib planks were placed on both sides of the post so the wheels could safely ride over it. The crew developed new respect for the quality of sign installation provided by Caltrans. Having lost about ten minutes of the schedule, the sign was left in its horizontal position.

It was just after 1:00 a.m. There were several drinking establishments along Alabama Avenue which had about a dozen customers. The array of flashing red and blue lights atop the lead CHP units attracted immediate attention on the quiet side street. When the huge fuselage loomed into view with attached American flags flying and the large, black-lettered words "United States of America" brightly lighted against the stark white background, it created quite a sensation. The pub patrons waved and cheered as the impromptu parade passed in review. Several who may have served in the armed forces showed their respect by standing at attention and giving military salutes.

This spectacle of Air Force One on a quiet street in San Bernardino in the middle of the night will likely be remembered and talked about by these witnesses for many years to come.

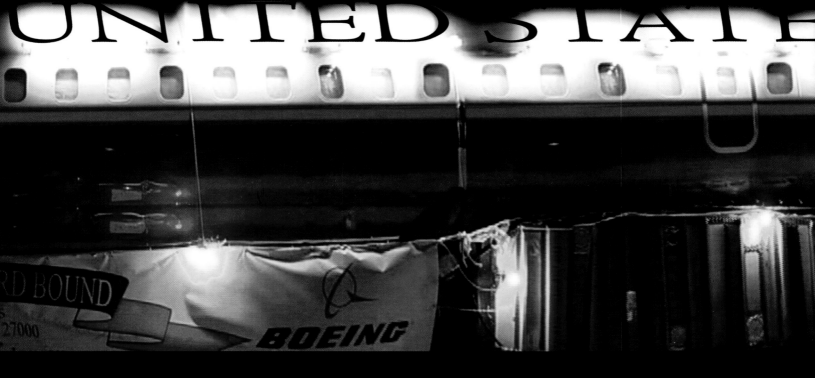

ON THE ROAD

At the 10 Freeway, the entourage entered the westbound lanes, which had been cleared of all traffic by the CHP.

According to Randy Huizenga, he mentally reviewed the many steps he and the assembled crew had taken to arrive at this point in the project. They had been working eighteen to twenty hours a day for nearly three weeks to accomplish the mission.

As the procession increased its speed to thirty miles an hour, Huizenga noted the bounce caused by the expansion joints in the concrete freeway that had the effect of mini speed bumps. He had no doubts about the ability of the Peterbilt he was driving. It was a solid

machine designed to haul extremely heavy loads. The 65,000-pound fuselage was well within its capabilities. He watched as the CHP lead units cleared traffic ahead while the rear units kept the curious at a safe distance. Meanwhile, the camera van maneuvered around the fuselage to capture images of the surrealistic scene of Air Force One traveling along a freeway in Southern California.

The transition to the northbound 215 Freeway was smooth. A few vehicles were parked on overpasses to watch. Despite efforts to maintain a low profile about the move, several news media outlets provided the route and estimated times of the procession. After a few miles, the route switched to the westbound 210 Freeway, which would comprise the longest stretch on one freeway.

Everything was going remarkably smooth as Huizenga shifted to lower gears while climbing the grade through La Cañada Flintridge along the foothills of the majestic San Gabriel Mountains. A light mist began to bead against the windshield of the large tractor as Huizenga heard a "pop" and noticed vibration in the steering wheel. He turned to Bob David and said evenly, "I think we might have blown a tire." Bob replied, "You're kidding. Everything was going so well."

Huizenga radioed Chris Mollno in the pilot truck and told him what had happened. Chris replied that there was an area a few miles ahead that would provide a good place to pull off the freeway.

Since everyone in the procession monitored the same radio frequency, all knew immediately about the blowout. Manuel Rodriquez, who drove the tire change vehicle, started his air compressor so he would have full pressure by the time his rig pulled to the side of the freeway. Chris radioed to Huizenga that the pullover would be in two miles, just passed the Ocean View Boulevard exit. He said to pull off as far as possible so traffic would be allowed to pass.

As the rig pulled off and the CHP opened the lanes, vehicles that had been blocked about a quarter of a mile behind the fuselage finally got the chance to see why there was a major traffic control operation in the wee hours of June 21. Drivers slowed to get a good look at 27000 as she sat on the side of the roadway.

Manuel pulled his utility truck beside the rig and jumped out of the cab to examine the damaged tire located on the inside rear quadrant of the right wheel assembly. The tire was shredded. Fortunately, the other seven tires were strong enough to absorb the added weight. Manuel grabbed an air-driven lug wrench hooked by hose to his onboard compressor. In a matter of minutes, he had

the rim off its axle and had removed the damaged tire. He placed a new tire on the rim, inflated it, and installed it on the axle hub. CHP officers watched in amazement as the tire mechanic applied his craft. In less than ten minutes, the job was completed. One officer commented that the mechanic should be on a NASCAR racing team. Huizenga added that Manuel was a well-regarded professional and was selected because of his reputation among truckers in the heavy hauling industry.

Quickly, everyone got back in their vehicles as the CHP units down the freeway pulled out to create a traffic break. Once the rig was back in the double lanes it occupied, the rolling traffic control continued on the 210 Freeway to its connection with the Ronald Reagan 118 Freeway that crosses the San Fernando Valley. At the western end of the valley, the freeway rises through a boulder-strewn area called Rocky Peak, where many Western movies were filmed.

Huizenga called the pilot truck and said he had to make a stop. Not asking why, Chris Mollno pulled to the side of the freeway. Watching his rearview mirror, Chris saw Huizenga jump down from the cab and disappear a short distance off the road. He reappeared in a few moments, climbed into the idling cab, and pulled the rig onto the road.

"What was that?" radioed one of the CHP officers. Huizenga quickly responded, "Too much coffee."

About seven miles west of Rocky Peak was the Cochran Street Bridge—the lowest obstacle on the 102-mile odyssey. As they approached the bridge, Chris, in the pilot truck, pulled to the far left lane and radioed to Huizenga that the clearance was highest at the center. Slowing to about ten miles per hour, Huizenga maneuvered the rig until his tractor's left wheels were on the center shoulder aligned with the highest point of the bridge and then braked to a stop. Several on the support crew quickly jumped from their vehicles and went to the hydraulic piston assembly that supported the nose of the fuselage. When a release valve was opened, escaping air pressure caused the piston to slowly lower on its shaft nearly six inches, creating the clearance needed to safely pass under the bridge. Trusting the measurements provided by the Permit Company, Huizenga hauled 27000 under the bridge with less than six inches clearance from the top of the fuselage. Once clear, the rig was stopped for an application of air pressure that caused the support mechanism to rise to its full extension. Huizenga took a deep breath and slowly accelerated to thirty miles an hour.

When asked how he knew the load would clear since he had never driven this route before, Huizenga explained that it's all a team effort among the pilot, the driver, the rigging company, and a little luck. "We try to eliminate Murphy's Law as much as is humanly possible."

As they approached the Madera Road exit, the destination was now within a few miles, everyone began to relax with the knowledge that most of the challenge had been met—except for Presidential Drive.

PRESIDENTIAL RETROSPECTIVES

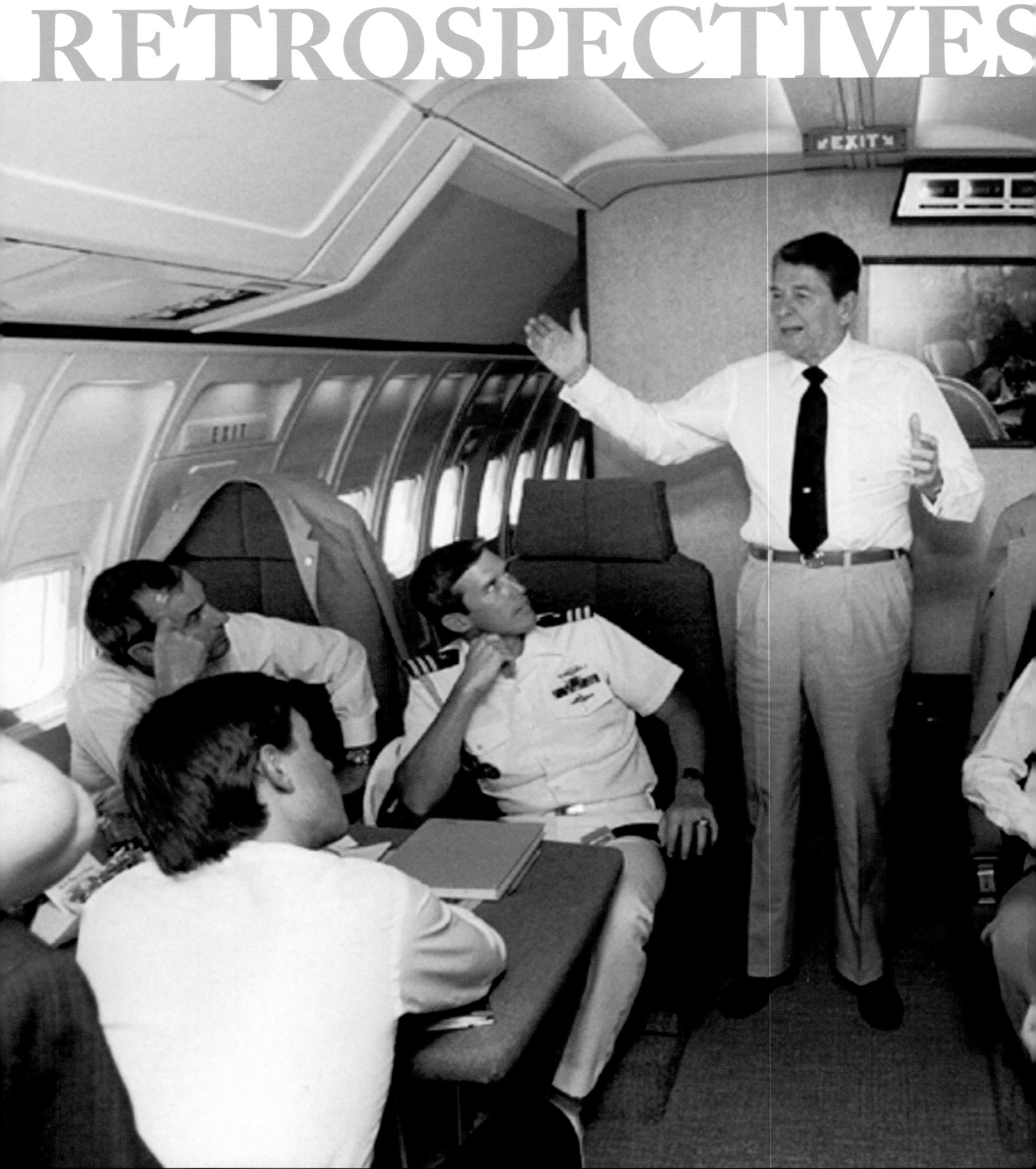

An airborne White House, with worldwide strategic air command capabilities, it's a better office than any I have. I can get more done on this plane. For example, I do a lot of letter writing…a lot of mail that I choose to answer myself. I can get on this plane and on a trip, I can come back with a tablet full and all the letters attached to it and hand it in to the office to be typed for my signature.

There is instant communication and not only with the White House, but many times there have been international conversations from this plane and on a secure phone.

When you're abroad and in strange lands and you've been there and you're very busy and then you arrive back at the airport and your first glimpse of this plane and that flag up there, yes, it's a little bit like hearing the National Anthem and you swell a little with pride.

Ronald Reagan

PRESIDENT

As Randy Huizenga approached Presidential Drive, which would be a hard right turn off of Madera Road, he swung the rig to the far left side of the roadway so he would be perfectly aligned for the final lap of the move.

As he did, a call came on the radio that he should stop once his load had cleared Madera Road and hold his position until further notice.

The CHP units had accomplished their mission of escorting and protecting Air Force One on the freeway system. After a round of handshakes, the patrol officers sped off to find breakfast.

Nearly two hours later, with the early morning sun beginning to lighten the low cloud cover over Simi Valley, the call came over the radio to proceed. Huizenga had used the time to walk up the road to see the extent of the hill-climbing challenge.

The one-mile-long drive snakes up a swatch cut into the hills overlooking Simi Valley and the Los Padres National Forest. It reaches nearly a 5 percent grade as it ascends over five hundred feet to the Library. Popular with fitness runners, Presidential Drive provides athletes with the kind of rapid elevation not found on many roads in the area.

Huizenga warned his entourage, that once this rig weighing nearly fifty tons got moving up Presidential Drive, there was nothing for which he was going to stop. He had discovered during test runs at the airport that the way the structural supports were constructed, they wouldn't allow for backing down the hill. Even with a supercharged engine and the low gearing of the long-nosed Peterbilt, once forward motion was lost, it would be practically impossible to start again from a dead stop on that steep of an incline.

Another thought crossed Huizenga's mind. All those welded attachments he had made to the crew's designs would be put to their most severe test. It is one thing to run on a flat surface, but a steep climb shoves all the stress to the limits of tolerance. If he had to stop and try to start again, the torque of the engine might cause something to give. If Murphy's Law were going to kick in, this hill would provide the opportunity.

Firing up the diesel, Huizenga set the gearshift lever and released the clutch, engaging the transmission. With the supercharger winding up to a shrill and heavy smoke chuffing from the twin exhaust pipes, Air Force One inched forward on her last lap as a moving vehicle. The first few hundred yards were rather easy for the tractor to gain speed following Presidential Drive since it swung easterly around a gentle curve then up a gradual left arc accompanied by increased grade. As the fuselage emerged from the low-lying fog

that hugged the side of the Simi hills, it took on the appearance of a white-and-blue submarine surfacing in a white sea. From time to time, Air Force One disappeared under the billowing cover, only to resurface a few hundred feet farther up the grade.

Scanning his dashboard gauges for signs of trouble, Huizenga was satisfied that the engine's vital signs were functioning within their normal ranges. As the rig approached the steepest portion of the climb, a photographer was standing in the middle of the roadway snapping pictures with his camera. Huizenga leaned forward in his

hours, Huizenga climbed into the truck and started maneuvering the rig slowly back and forth until he aligned the fuselage with the tail facing the building. At one point, he pulled the tractor's front wheels so close to the cliff's edge that dirt gave way under their weight. Everyone watched in amazement as the twenty-year veteran trucker finessed the rig into what everyone agreed was the right position— where she would stay for nearly two years through rain, wind, and fire while awaiting her new home on the hill.

Without saying much, Huizenga grabbed his teddy bear and thermos and headed for the parking lot where he climbed into a pickup truck his brother had driven to the Library, and the two drove off. The next time he saw Air Force One was during the dedication ceremonies in September 2005.

PRESIDENTIAL RETROSPECTIVES

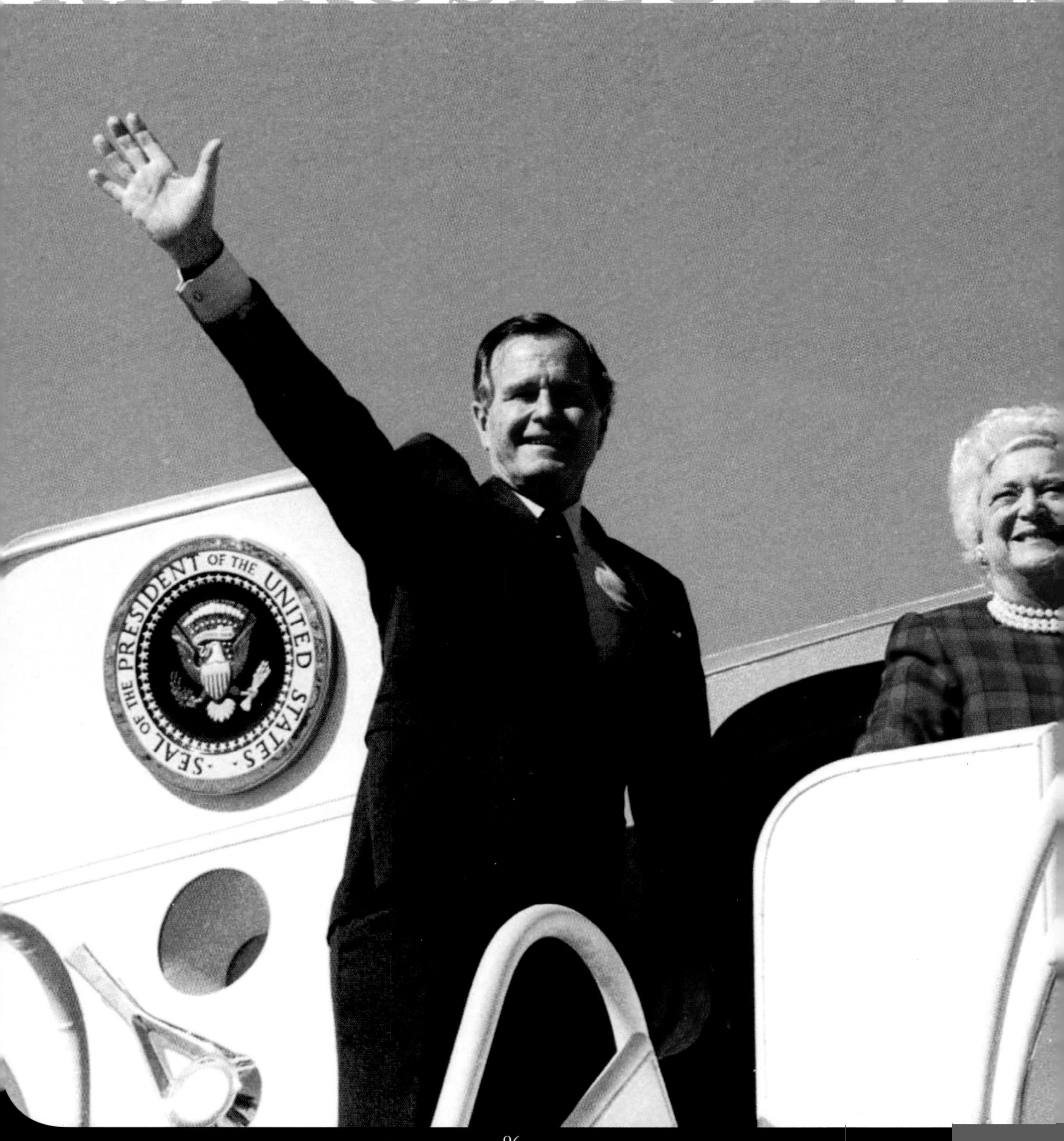

The American Presidency is an institution rich in symbolism, and outside the White House itself, certainly one of the most powerful icons of that high office is Air Force One. Indeed, Air Force One is probably the most visible global symbol of the Presidency. In that sense, it not only serves as a highly efficient mode of travel by a President and his staff—with its state-of-the-art communications and other modern necessities—it also projects American influence to our allies and adversaries around the world. Suffice it to say, I have fond memories of my travels aboard 27000, primarily during 1989 and 1990. It was cozier than the new class of 747s that followed, which came online during my Presidency, but it served our team very well—just as it did for the six other Commanders-in-Chief who rode it.

Barbara and I are very pleased it has found a permanent home at the Reagan Library, where it will serve as a vibrant, interactive, and instructive reminder of a memorable period in the life of our nation.

THE RONALD R

EARTH WIND & FIRE

The flashing red light behind the rearview mirror of Ventura County Fire Chief Bob Roper's blue Ford Crown Victoria cast an intermittent red hue over the covered fuselage and wings of 27000.

She was in open storage waiting for Air Force One Pavilion, which was just getting under construction about fifty feet away. On this night in late October 2003, an eerie amber glow highlighted the dark sky as thousands of acres of Ventura and Los Angeles counties were being consumed in one of the worst wildfires in Southern California history.

In a process repeated annually, the brush surrounding the Reagan Presidential Library had been cleared to eliminate the fuel that fed these perennial wildfires. Unfortunately, in a major conflagration, live embers can be carried over a mile on currents of hot wind created within the firestorm, starting new fires in a leapfrog pattern across the landscape.

Having been relocated to the Library that spring, Air Force One was a new responsibility for the Ventura County Fire Department. Chief Roper personally drove to the site from his command headquarters in Camarillo to measure the potential threat from the fire and to examine conditions surrounding the plane. His department had a close working relationship with the Reagan Foundation and provided volunteer crews to maintain the brush clearance around the Library. He wanted to be certain Ventura County's newest celebrity resident was going to be safe.

The veteran firefighter's recommendation to the project manager of the plane and Pavilion, who met the chief as he got out of his vehicle, was to remove the fabric cover from the plane. A fire-

retardant cover had been ordered to protect the plane, but there hadn't been enough time to get delivery.

The chief explained that he had ordered four pumper fire trucks and an aircraft foaming truck to be deployed to the site. He said the plane's survival chances were far greater if the cover wasn't in place to trap live embers that were beginning to fall in the area.

"Our firefighters can douse a metal surface with water or foam much more efficiently without the fabric cover," Roper advised.

The crew was directed to pull the cover and get it away from the aircraft. Fortuately, the wings had been drained and purged of aviation fuel back in 2001 when 27000 first arrived in San Bernardino. The chief determined, "They shouldn't present a hazard."

Soon, several large pumper trucks pulled onto the plateau that had been created below the main Library and Museum buildings. Firefighters climbed quickly from their rigs and began pulling canvas hoses and laying lines to the fuselage and wings. Charging the high-pressure hoses with water from onboard tanks, the firefighters tested the flow at the nozzles. A short time later, an aircraft crash truck arrived from its base at Camarillo Airport. The top-mounted high-pressure foaming nozzle was aimed at the fuselage. When or if the firestorm tried to take the hill, Ventura County firefighting personnel and their equipment would be ready.

A crew from KABC-TV News and photographers from the *Los Angeles Times* and the *Ventura County Star* appeared at the Library and filmed the silhouette of the fuselage against a wall of flames. With telephoto lenses, their pictures made it appear as though the fire in the background was quite near the site when, in fact, it was a mile to the east. Pictures on national television and in the next morning's newspapers prompted telephone calls to the fire department's dispatch center and to the Reagan Foundation from concerned citizens throughout the country. Callers were assured that firefighters and their equipment were on the site and prepared to defend Air Force One. In addition, fire retardant solution could have been dropped by Ventura County Fire Department helicopters had the situation become more threatening.

This became unnecessary when cooling breezes from the Pacific Ocean began to tame the westerly advance of the fire line, pushing it north and east and eventually quelling the damaging and deadly fire. Driven by hot, dry Santa Ana winds throughout Southern California that fall, the firestorm blackened more than 743,000 acres and destroyed 3,570 dwellings. Twenty-two deaths were attributed to the series of wildfires, which included some set by arsonists.

The Reagan Foundation and the crew had assumed getting Air Force One delivered to the Library undamaged was going to be their major challenge. They never imagined that they and a team of twenty-seven firefighters would be standing sentry over the plane throughout the night while much of the countryside they could view from their vantage point was in flames.

Photo by Glenn Grossman

A week later, it began to rain.

That winter became one of the wettest in more than one hundred years. A series of storms soaked the ground throughout Southern California, causing new concerns about flooding and landslides below burned areas. In fact, the following two years continued the wet trend as massive shifts in the stratospheric jet stream caused storms to drift south of their usual track.

Long recognized as a desert plain, Southern California had become urbanized with huge housing tracts, golf courses, business parks, and shopping malls connected by a lattice of freeways. With development, landscaping brought in trees, lawns, and shrubs.

The terrain and the weather were changing. The region was entering a twenty-year cycle of wet winters— just in time for the construction of Air Force One Pavilion.

PRESIDENTIAL
RETROSPECTIVES

The advent of air travel transformed the scope of the American presidency, and the jet deemed "27000" ushered our nation into its leading position on the global playing field. In transporting seven Presidents around the world, Air Force One 27000 bore witness to history. President Ronald Reagan travelled far and wide to spread his message of freedom and hope, and it's only fitting that the aircraft has retired to the warmth of his beloved California. This book allows the reader a rare look at an extraordinary part of America's past.

Bill Clinton

May 1, 2006

PAVILION ON THE HILL

Seven architectural firms were invited by the Reagan Foundation to present concepts for an Air Force One Pavilion to be built adjacent to the Ronald Reagan Presidential Library and Museum in the hills above Simi Valley.

Out of the creative crucible that ensued over several months, one firm emerged with a concept that proposed to create a memorable presentation of an American treasure while preserving the Presidential dignity of the aircraft. In the opinion of the Reagan Foundation's building committee, chaired by Los Angeles business leader Robert Tuttle, the challenge was met by Clinger Spina Associates (CSA) located in the Westwood area of Los Angeles near the campus of UCLA. With the committee's recommendation, the Foundation's board of directors was given a presentation by CSA featuring a detailed scale model and computer-animated visual renderings of the exterior and interior of the proposed building.

The presentation highlighted how the plane would be displayed and how visitors would enter the building in a way that would create maximum dramatic impact. A term that became popular in describing the approaching view of the plane was the "Castle Effect," meaning the view Walt Disney created at Disneyland from Main Street USA toward Sleeping Beauty Castle. "It created a point of reference for guests at the themed amusement park, the same objective we had here," said Duke Blackwood, executive director of the Reagan Foundation.

Also of importance in the design was that the additional building would integrate harmoniously with the existing campus. The new building would not intrude on the serene setting or create visual impairment to the rolling terrain. Their demonstration of understanding and interpreting the mission of the new structure resulted in CSA being awarded the design contract.

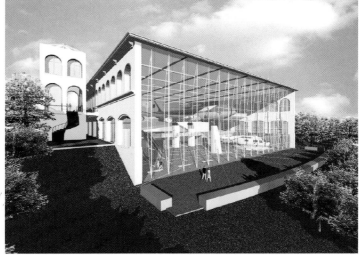

The Museum of Presidential Travel
RONALD REAGAN PRESIDENTIAL FOUNDATION

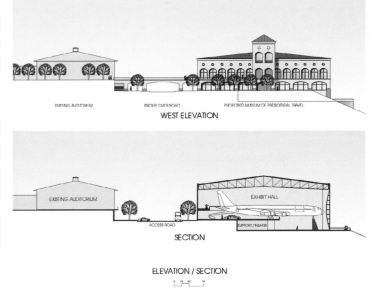

The Museum of Presidential Travel
RONALD REAGAN PRESIDENTIAL FOUNDATION

"We looked at several buildings, such as the National Aeronautics and Space Museum in Washington, D.C., and the building that once housed Howard Hughes's Spruce Goose in Long Beach," explained Daniel Clinger, principal and director of design for CSA. "We realized this was a unique project and an unusual opportunity to design a building that would be for the ages."

According to Clinger, they had an additional challenge because the site was uneven with fill earth on one side and a fairly flat area on the other side. It required engineering of the terrain to prepare for a stable foundation. Of critical importance was the method to support the 160,000-pound weight of the aircraft.

"We used three drilled pilings or caissons that were secured five feet into solid bedrock beneath the structural slab. Even if the soil subsided under the slab, the building would still stand since the foundation and the structure rest on the caissons," Clinger said.

Being in Southern California, the standards required for stability in a major earthquake are strict. The values of code requirements were increased ten times over the prior codes after the disastrous 1994 Northridge earthquake.

✪ PAVILION ON THE HILL ✪

The huge window on the northeast wall of the building is an engineering marvel.

"We came up with the idea, which is unique to this project. It utilizes vertical bow trusses, which support the glass panels that in turn bear the wind load," Clinger continued. "The trusses are tied together with cables side to side. The structure itself provides the rigidity for the window opening."

The major truss expands with the roof and is actually a lateral resisting member. Each five-foot-by-twelve-foot-six-inch rubber-insulated panel can move independently. An engineering consultant named Michael Griffin was hired to provide specific input for the window, which is 60 feet high and 180 feet wide with 168 laminated glass panels. The window is designed to withstand winds in excess of seventy miles an hour. Cleaning the glass was a major concern. After several engineering and design considerations, it was decided that the most practical solution was bringing in scaffolding twice a year and manually cleaning the glass.

The idea of giving the plane a kinetic effect by raising the nose twenty-eight inches higher than the tail came from architect Daniel Clinger. "Instead of being static, the subtle tilt gives the plane energy it wouldn't have otherwise." In actuality, the three-point mounted display of the aircraft inside a custom-built structure was unique in aviation. Most aircraft are simply displayed parked on a hard surface or on low pylons. Smaller aircraft are often suspended by cables from ceilings. Convenient public access to the interior of Air Force One was of major importance to the Reagan Foundation.

John A. Martin & Associates of Los Angeles provided structural engineering of the Pavilion and worked closely with CSA to ensure the 87,000-square-foot structure was properly designed for construction by Hathaway Dinwiddie, the noted building firm responsible for the Transamerica Pyramid in San Francisco and the Getty Museum in West Los Angeles. The 200-by-200-foot building utilized open span construction like that of an aircraft hangar. The columns around the walls and the roof beams work together to create a lateral resisting frame that does not require support within the building. This design allowed for one of the fifty-foot wall sections between two support columns to be left unfinished to permit the loading of Air Force One into the building.

At one point, it was planned that a fighter aircraft would be suspended by cables from the ceiling above the 707 as a defender. That idea required a structure that would support a heavy load hanging from its beams. Although the 30,000-pound F-14 Tomcat provided by the Navy Department was eventually placed outside the building next to the Peace Plaza, the option remains that rather heavy objects could be hung inside the Pavilion. Once 27000 was installed, though, it became apparent that the addition of another aircraft would have distracted from the dramatic impact of Air Force One.

The Marine One helicopter was located on the bottom floor to give the main stage to the 707. Also displayed on the main floor, under the right wing of Air Force One, are the armored Cadillac Presidential limousine used by the President and Mrs. Reagan in the early 1980s, a Secret Service black SUV, a Los Angeles Police Department black-and-white patrol car, and two police motorcycles donated by the Los Angeles Police Historical Society. They are staged ready to pull into position on the other side of Air Force One to receive the President as he deplanes.

United Technologies, which developed microturbines at its facility in Chatsworth, California, manufactured the heating and air conditioning system, which was engineered by Syska Hennessy. Together, they built a cogeneration plant with sixteen 60-kilowatt natural gas–fired turbines that produce enough capacity to carry the total electrical and air conditioning load of the entire Library. It was designed to produce enough electricity to sustain the Library without support from the power grid.

The budget was constantly a challenge as material costs escalated during construction. Steel increased 40 percent during the period from October 2003 when site work commenced to the dedication ceremonies in late October 2005.

In all, the building required twenty thousand cubic yards of earth to be moved, fifty-six hundred cubic yards of concrete to be poured, and 757 tons of steel to create the structure. More than three hundred design and engineering drawings guided the construction.

PRESIDENTIAL RETROSPECTIVES

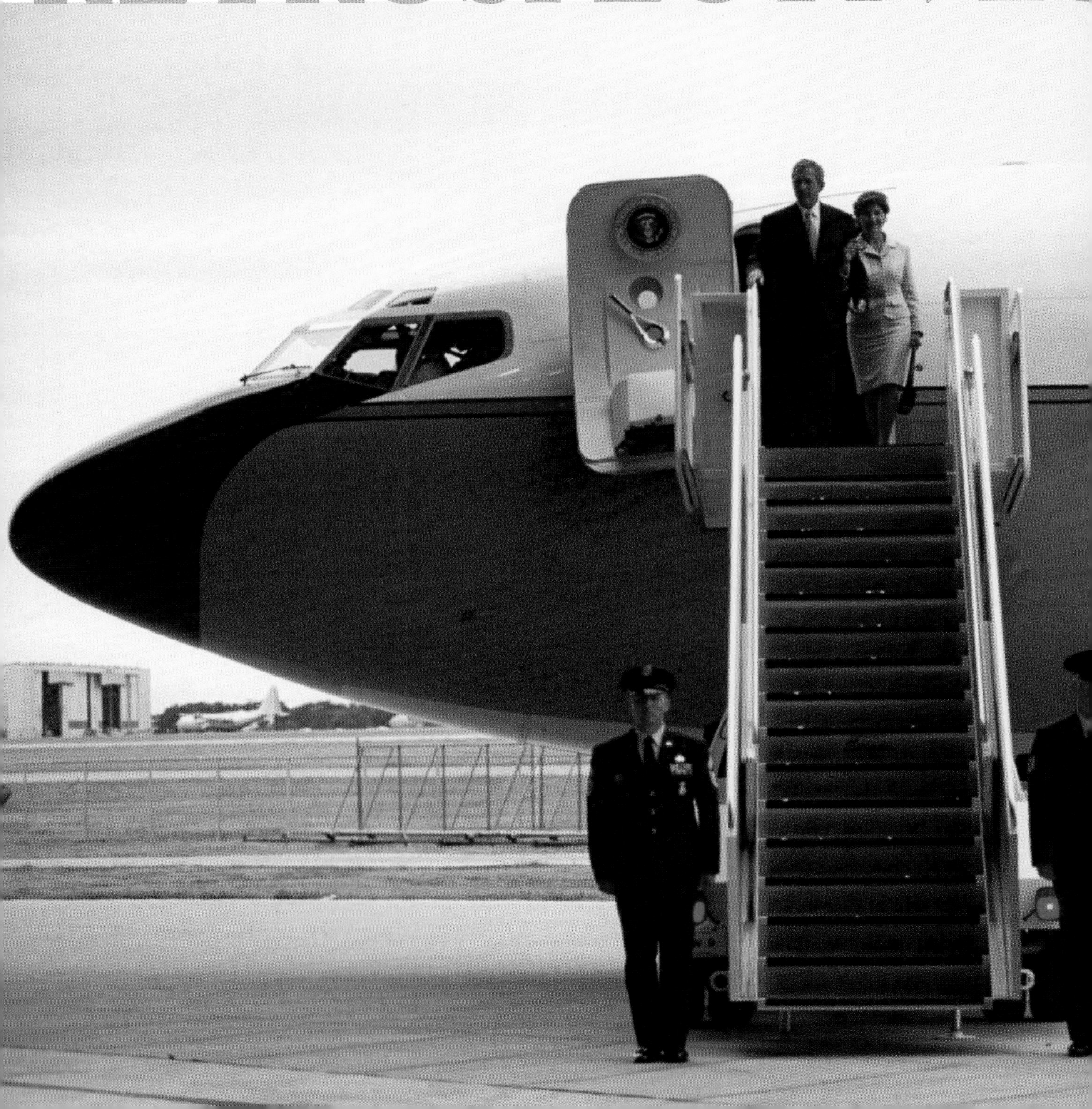

Any Air Force plane carrying the President bears the name Air Force One. This plane, tail number 27000, wore the name of Air Force One for 444 missions and more than one million miles. Today this plane carried a President for the last time, and soon it will be taking its last flight.

It will carry no more presidents, but it will carry forever the spirit of American democracy. Tail number 27000 entered the service of the United States in December 1972, and first served President Richard Nixon, and then President Ford. It flew former President Carter and former Vice President Mondale to Germany, to greet fifty-two Americans who had been held hostage in Iran.

My father flew it frequently, but the President who used it the most was Ronald Reagan. It was from this plane that President Reagan disembarked in Berlin in 1987 and demanded, "Mr. Gorbachev, tear down this wall." And none of those flights would have been possible without the skill and commitment of the aircrews of old 27000.

For almost three decades, the pilot and crew of tail number 27000 have performed flawlessly. Tail number 27000 flew two Presidents back home from Washington to California—it carried Richard Nixon in 1974 and Ronald Reagan in 1989.

And today, it will follow its distinguished passengers to its own retirement in California. A new hangar will be built for 27000 at the Reagan Library in Simi Valley, California. Visitors will soon be able to tour this aircraft. It will remind us of Ronald Reagan's achievements for peace and international security and permanently symbolize the soaring spirit of this great man and our great country. Soon it will take its final flight westward into history.

Bush Bush

August 29, 2001

AIRSHIP IN A BOTTLE

After waiting fifteen months for the Pavilion to be far enough along in construction, the day approached for 27000 to move into her new permanent home overlooking Simi Valley.

The plan was to install the plane before completing the last section of the southwest wall.

Three large seismic-isolated pedestals had been constructed to support 27000 at her landing gear points. These reinforced-concrete-and-steel caissons were anchored five feet into solid bedrock below

the foundation of the Pavilion. Independent of the structure of the building, they were designed to support the 160,000-pound weight of the craft with contact limited to the landing gear. The support for the nose gear extended twenty-five feet above the lower floor of the Pavilion. The two pedestals for the main landing gear extended seven feet above the cantilevered upper floor. An observation walkway that was even with the plane created a half circle facing the wall of glass. The tops of the two pedestals on the upper floor were slightly shorter than the nose gear pedestal to give 27000 a two-degree incline toward the sky beyond the horizon over the rolling hills.

The challenge was to get the plane inside the building, reassembled, and positioned on the elevated pedestals. Project manager Bob David relied on the expertise of Coast Machinery Movers, which handled the plane's move from San Bernardino. The fuselage was resting on large jack stands that had replaced the quad-wheeled supports used during the move from San Bernardino International Airport. The two wings were stored next to it where they were originally deposited on the open plateau about fifty feet from the building. The positioning of the plane and wings was strategically planned for the move into the building. In the heat of the Southern California summer, members of the Boeing crew examined the wings and discovered the hollow structures provided ideal habitats for local wildlife, including mice, birds, and rattlesnakes.

After the critters were relocated to safer environs, each wing was hoisted onto a flatbed trailer by a pair of cranes and moved into the building via a fifty-foot gap in the unfinished southwest wall. They were strategically placed on the floor so they could be rejoined later to the fuselage. The front of the fuselage was then hooked to the front of a tractor provided by EZE Trucking Company. Another diesel tractor was hooked at the rear via cables fastened to the mover's dollies, which supported the plane where the main landing gear had been. With one tractor at the rear pulling and one facing the fuselage and pushing on the tow bar connected to the nose gear assembly, they slowly moved the fuselage backward toward the Library's loading dock located south of the Pavilion.

Once the fuselage was near the loading dock, the rear tractor was unhitched, and the front tractor pushed the plane until it practically touched the loading dock. At this point, a discussion ensued about how to maneuver the fuselage into the building. It was decided that the front tractor would be turned around so it faced the opening in the Pavilion. The angle from the loading dock required precise positioning so the dollies would clear steel supports that would later provide the base for structural columns used to complete the building.

Firing up the truck, the driver started slowly moving toward the opening and then cut his wheels to the right, allowing the fuselage to align perfectly. This maneuver caused the rear of the fuselage to swing to the left with the nose pointing toward the opening in the building.

At a cautious pace, the tractor towed the fuselage into the building where the sound of the powerful diesel engine echoed throughout the steel structure. It went so smoothly that it was decided that only a few additional "rehearsals" would be necessary to ensure that the procedure would be performed perfectly for a media event the next day featuring Nancy Reagan and Duke Blackwood, executive director of the Reagan Foundation, and other dignitaries.

After moving the fuselage out of the building and angling it slightly to the south, a second run commenced. However, this time the angle wasn't as precise, and the dolly under the right side headed directly for the steel supports on the side of the opening. After several attempts to correct the angle, it became apparent that the fuselage was hemmed in against the opening. A crane was moved into position and lifted the fuselage free of its predicament. Realizing the angle and the positioning of the tractor would have to follow a precise course, several more rehearsals were done until everyone was satisfied that the task could be duplicated without incident.

On September 21, 2004, Air Force One officially moved into the Air Force One Pavilion with appropriate celebration and media coverage. The maneuver was handled perfectly for the news cameras, which was reflected in Mrs. Reagan's approving smile as she signaled the crew to bring Air Force One home.

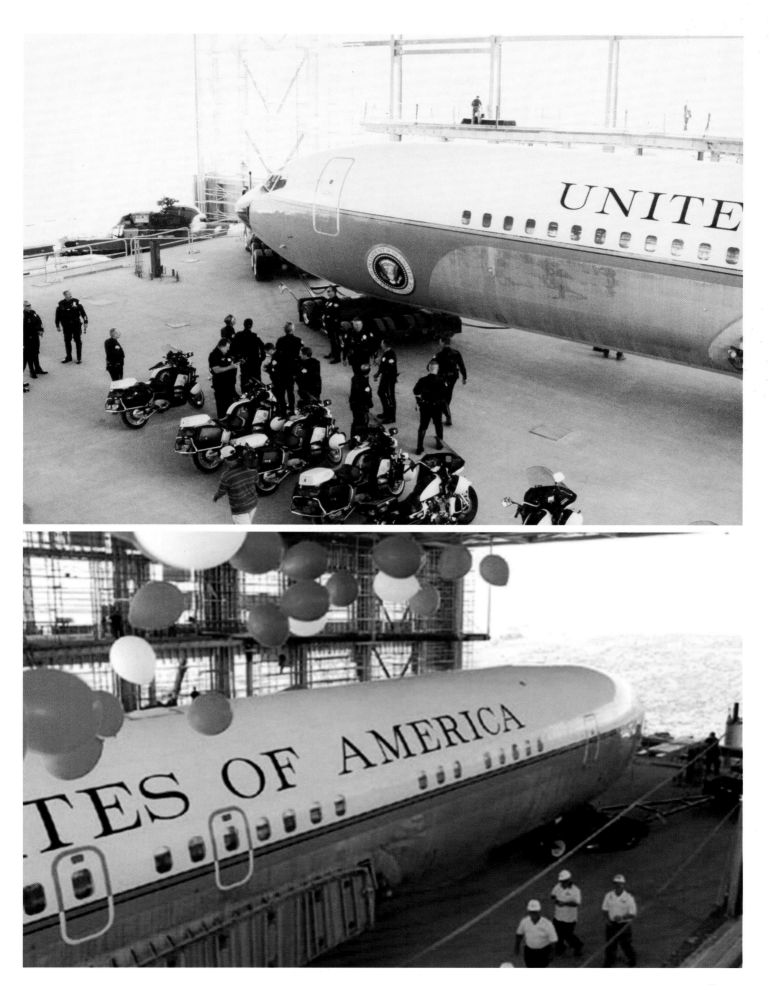

It had been a long journey, and the final steps were set in motion to secure the plane's future as an American treasure. Air Force One joined the Marine One Sikorsky helicopter, which already had been moved into the building earlier that morning. Since the copter would require major cosmetic restoration, its condition didn't warrant attention that day. It had seen years of duty, including service during President Johnson's era.

Casually looking at the huge fuselage and wings, and their intended positioning atop the three pedestals, begged the question: "How in the world was this going to be done?" The answer was found in strategy that rivaled construction of the ancient pyramids in Egypt.

The crew went to work, beginning with the installation of the original nose gear that had been removed to accommodate the wheeled structure engineered for the move. Next, a temporary bridge was constructed between the upper level concrete floor and the nose pedestal. This provided a pathway for the dual truck of the landing gear to ride on. Once the gear was in place, the fuselage was pushed halfway across the bridge and held in this position for the installation of the wings.

The portion of the fuselage remaining over the upper floor was lifted into cradles by large cranes, and the equipment used to haul it into the Pavilion was removed.

AIRSHIP IN A BOTTLE

Now that it was positioned for reassembly, the wings had to be reattached. Using two large cranes, the wings were hoisted into place for the Boeing crew, working on hydraulic manlifts, to reinsert the hundreds of fasteners required to hold each wing in place. The ends of the wings had to be raised to perfectly align the holes. Tripods equipped with bottle jacks were placed under the wings to provide additional support. Next, the four Pratt & Whitney turbine jet engines were reattached under the wings. This process went rather smoothly.

Work continued during this time to complete reattaching the remaining parts. The vertical stabilizer, or tail, was lifted by crane and reconnected to the fuselage. Next, the flaps were reconnected to the wings. At the same time, the horizontal stabilizers were hoisted by crane and reinstalled. Air Force One was beginning to look flightworthy again.

According to John Bouza of Boeing, attaching the landing gear was a major challenge that rivaled battlefield conditions because of the remote location of the Pavilion. Under normal circumstances, construction is performed at a plant designed to build aircraft where there are special tools available to accomplish this task. The landing gear is attached to new aircraft early in the process to provide a secure way to maneuver the structure during construction. Since there were no special tools available, such as a laser-guided device used to align the holes to attach the bolts, the crew had to improvise. The crew used their eyesight and best guesstimates of distance to match up the landing gear struts with the attachment points in the wells of the fuselage and wings.

A procedure that would usually take an hour or less in Boeing's plant stretched into more than a day and a half as the crew struggled to align the 4,600-pound landing gear precisely to the correct level using a forklift. After many tries, a final manual nudge by four perspiring crewmembers closed the elusive gap, allowing the main anchor bolts to be inserted. After this tiring learning process, the second landing gear installation took only a half-day. Because visitors would be walking under the plane, the integrity of the reassembly had to approach that of airworthiness.

❖ AIRSHIP IN A BOTTLE ❖

A long, steel I-beam girder was threaded under the main landing gear. Two heavy-duty bottle jacks were welded to the underside of the girder. When the jacks raised the girder about eight inches, a railroad tie was placed under the girder. The jacks were then raised again until there was clearance for another tie to be added under the beam. This process was repeated until the bottoms of the eight wheels of the main landing gear were even with the tops of the pedestals. At each end of the support I-beam, small dollies were attached. Two I-beams mounted on bottle jacks were positioned underneath the dollies at right angles facing the window, creating channels for the dollies to roll on when the plane got its final push into place.

At the same time the rear of the fuselage was being raised, the front of the plane also had to be aligned with the single pedestal for the nose gear.

The steel girders used to construct the temporary bridge for the nose gear to ride on between the cantilevered upper floor and the front pedestal were supported on an I-beam-and-jack assembly located on the lower floor. To secure the plane, a webbed sling was placed over the forward area of the fuselage. When activated, the jacks lifted the front of the plane to align it with the front pedestal at the same time the main landing gear was being raised level with the two rear pedestals.

Once all the landing gear was aligned with each pedestal, the plane was carefully moved forward by a large forklift and positioned onto the three pedestals. With the plane finally sitting on its new perch, the nose gear was bolted to its mount, and the main landing gear was bolted and welded to the two main pedestal mounts. The crew seemed relieved that this monumental task was completed without mishap.

BI 40

However, before anyone could fully relax, what sounded like the loud crack of a rifle shot echoed throughout the building. At the same time, the plane shuttered and slumped suddenly toward the right, causing the starboard wing to move up and down.

A quick inspection revealed that the center tubular structure between the front and rear axles of the right landing gear assembly had cracked in half where it had been welded a few hours earlier to an anchor brace designed to hold the gear on the pedestal. An observer commented that it's not normal procedure to weld together two different alloys in high-stress applications because the extreme heat of the torch changes the tensile strength of the metals. It turned out that the metal used to construct the landing gear was of a different composition than that of the anchor brace.

Several hours later, while discussions continued regarding the best method to fix the broken landing gear, a second loud crack reverberated throughout the building as the plane shifted in the opposite direction with even more violence, causing both wings to flap. Everyone under the plane quickly scattered in all directions, not knowing in the next moment if the entire plane was going to come crashing down to the split level concrete floor, which likely would have cut the fuselage in half.

After a few anxious moments, the crew cautiously began to draw back into the building. Everything was extremely quiet except for the sound of the wind that almost continuously stirred the air around the Pavilion. Outside, a red-tailed hawk occasionally made a screech while turning lazy circles looking for prey. Other than that, the scene was silent.

Quickly realizing that the plane had to be stabilized, the long support I-beam was reinserted under the landing gear. After several meetings, Hales Engineering in Camarillo, California, which had a well-established reputation for aeronautical engineering, was contracted to build replacement mounts. This took about two months to complete.

Because of the broken landing gear, Cliff Richards of Flightline Services from Augusta, Georgia, had to halt his work restoring the exterior finish of Air Force One. He took the opportunity to completely disassemble the landing gear struts and meticulously painted each piece. The parts were strung like bones on a clothesline between the stacks of railroad ties supporting the I-beam. When the landing gear was reassembled, they looked brand new.

The day they arrived from Hales Engineering, the new mounts were installed on the pedestals and bolted to new landing gear trucks provided by Boeing. After a detailed inspection, the mounts were declared to be stable.

Richards and his two technicians, Scott Conley and Brian Simons, went back to work restoring the cosmetic look of the famous aircraft. The Raymond Loewy paint scheme had had numerous coatings and revisions to the original design applied over twenty-eight years of active service as Air Force One and as an "executive aircraft" for government officials. Mrs. Reagan wanted the plane to look exactly as it did when it served her husband.

The correct color palette and design were obtained from the Eighty-ninth Military Airlift Wing at Andrews Air Force Base in Maryland. One consideration was the aluminum frames that originally outlined the windows. They were no longer made and had been covered over when 27000 was reassigned from Air Force One to executive aircraft status. Richards said he could re-create the look of the original frames by using a special aluminum paint, which he successfully did.

He also spent many hours re-creating the official USAF markings and the military star and stripe symbols. Viewed on the plane, the markings didn't appear to be very large. In actuality, the size of Air Force One dwarfed them. For example, the USAF mark was fifteen feet long. The marks were carefully re-created by using layered stencils. Each layer revealed the plane's surface, providing perfect registration for the application of sprayed-on colors. In the case of the American flag on the vertical stabilizer, the paint crew worked on a manlift fifty feet above the floor, applying each of the colors until a perfect design was revealed when the last stenciled layer was peeled away.

They took special care to restore the bright finish of the polished aluminum skin by applying three different buffing steps from course to fine, followed by an application of wax to prevent the aluminum from oxidizing.

The most distinguishing feature of the livery was the huge "UNITED STATES OF AMERICA" lettered in black across both sides of the fuselage. Richards began its restoration by carefully cutting a mask for each letter. After doing so, the crew sprayed black paint over the masks. Then they removed the cutouts of the letters and sprayed black paint again, resulting in a perfect re-creation of the original lettering. After this, they replaced the masks over the letters, removed the surrounding material and sprayed the white finish of the roof of the plane. When completed, it looked exactly as it did twenty-eight years before, when Air Force One rolled out of the Boeing plant.

Concern for the overall finish of the plane induced the paint crew to take precautions against construction dust and paint overspray. As the finish on each section of the plane was completed, protective plastic sheeting was applied. Eventually, the entire aircraft was wrapped in layers of plastic like a giant present.

Once the glass panels were installed in the huge window wall, It was recommended that the glass be covered with plastic sheeting to protect it from paint overspray. Richards had learned his restoration skills by working in his late father's automobile repair shop, Richards Body Works, in Augusta, Georgia. Richards's brother still operates the business. These skills he refined by restoring aircraft since 1990 when his first project won an award. Since then, his reputation for aircraft restoration has led to many commissions throughout the country for military and private aircraft.

Restoring Marine One to its former glory was quite a challenge. When the Sikorsky CH 46-A arrived at the Library, it had seen much better days. Leaking hydraulic fluid from the rotor assembly covered much of the body. After cleaning with solvent, applying new paint, replacing the Plexiglas windows, and cleansing the cockpit, the appearance looked close to Presidential quality, at least on its surface.

The final exterior touch to Air Force One was the removal of the protective plastic sheets and the application of the Presidential Seal to the forward section of each side of the fuselage. Cliff Richards and one of his Flightline technicians, who expertly applied the huge adhesive decals, did this from a manlift. First, a soapy solution was put on the plane. Then the two-section vinyl decal was affixed. Using a small squeegee, they smoothed the decal until it laid flat against the surface of the aluminum skin with nary a wrinkle. If applied to the plane for flight service, the decals would have received a coating of clear polyurethane. In this case, it wasn't required.

While the exterior was getting most of the attention, the interior was being carefully renovated, cleaned, and prepared for visitors. Details of the interior were to reflect the time of the Reagan administration. A call went out for an IBM Selectric typewriter in the correct shade of blue. One was found, and it was donated to the Foundation.

Mrs. Reagan directed that access must accommodate the mobility impaired. The aisle through the plane was quite narrow. First, a section of seating along one wall was removed. This helped but didn't provide enough clearance for a standard wheelchair. Chief of Staff Joanne Drake suggested a narrow-wheeled apparatus that could transport a visitor through the plane. Someone discovered that

the airlines already had such a wheelchair, and two were ordered. A lift was installed so standard wheelchairs could be hoisted to the front entrance of the plane. In addition to a stairway, an elevator was already planned for the exit of the plane. Mrs. Reagan told the members of the Foundation that access for all was very important because it reflected the standards her husband held during his two terms in office in California as governor and his two terms as President.

Curious about the accuracy of the installation, the project manager measured the clearance of the plane with the mezzanine walkway and the gangway from the rear hatch to the elevator. He found the space between the structures and the plane was about one-eighth of an inch. Rather close considering the variations possible in both the plane and her new home on the hill.

It will challenge visitors to figure out how Air Force One got into the building and onto the pedestals—much like the enigma of a ship in a bottle.

PRESIDENTIAL RETROSPECTIVES

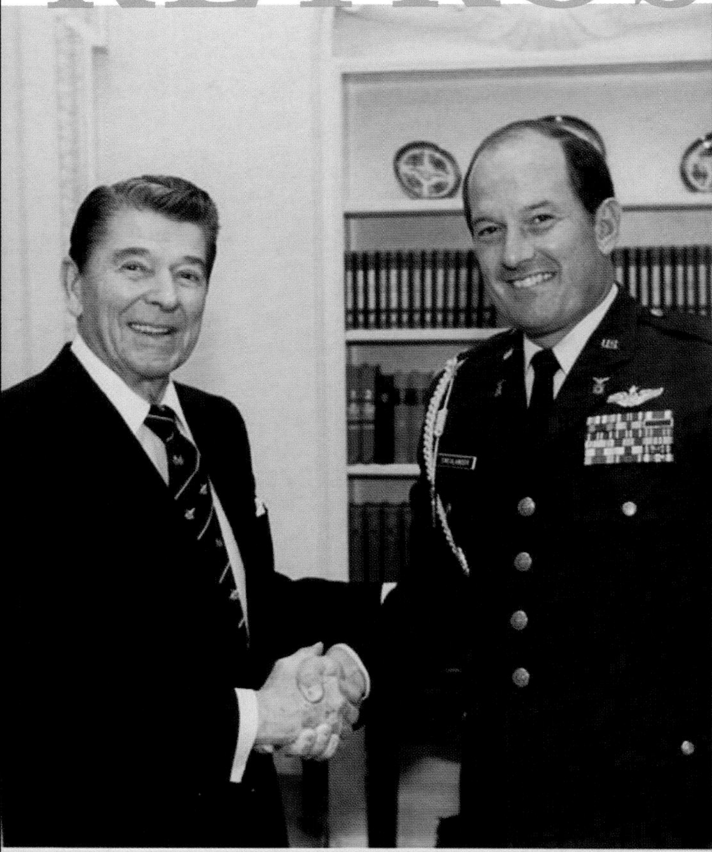

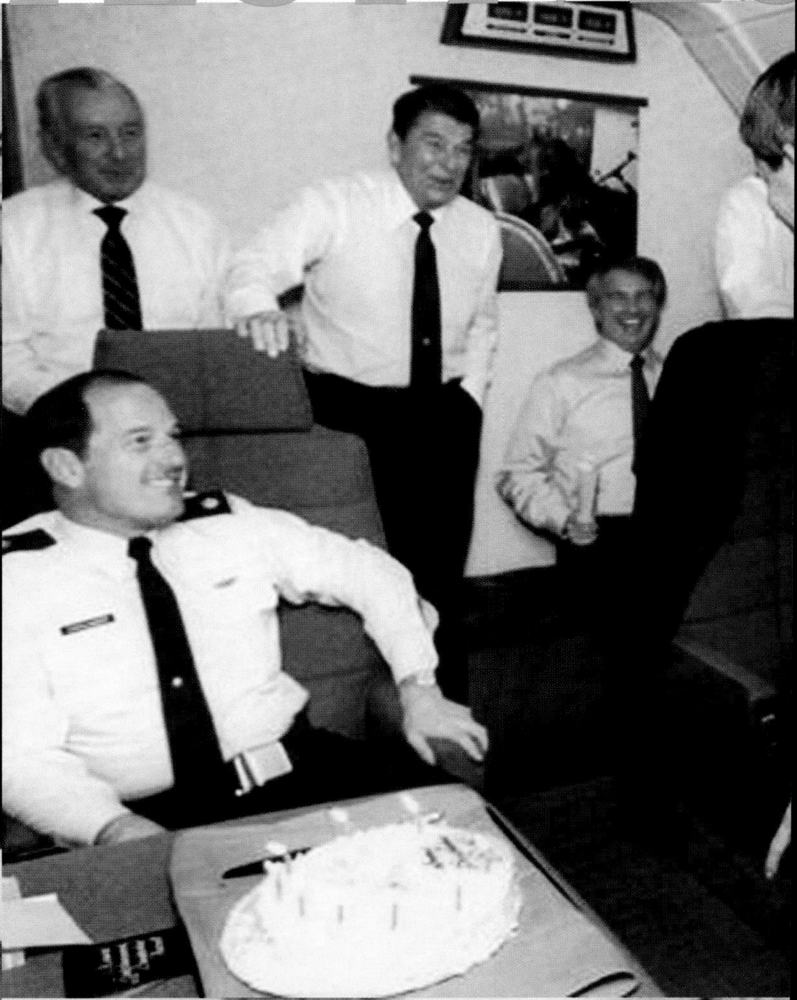

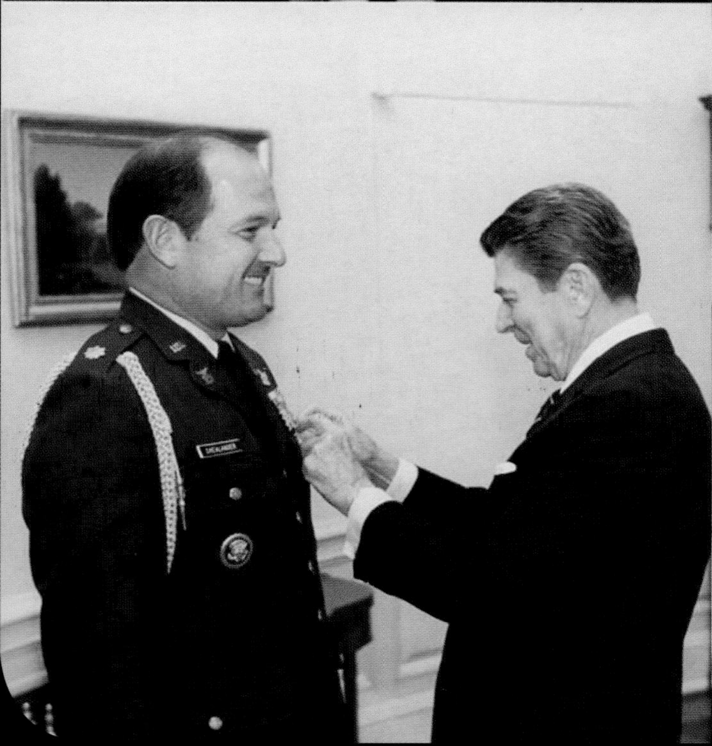

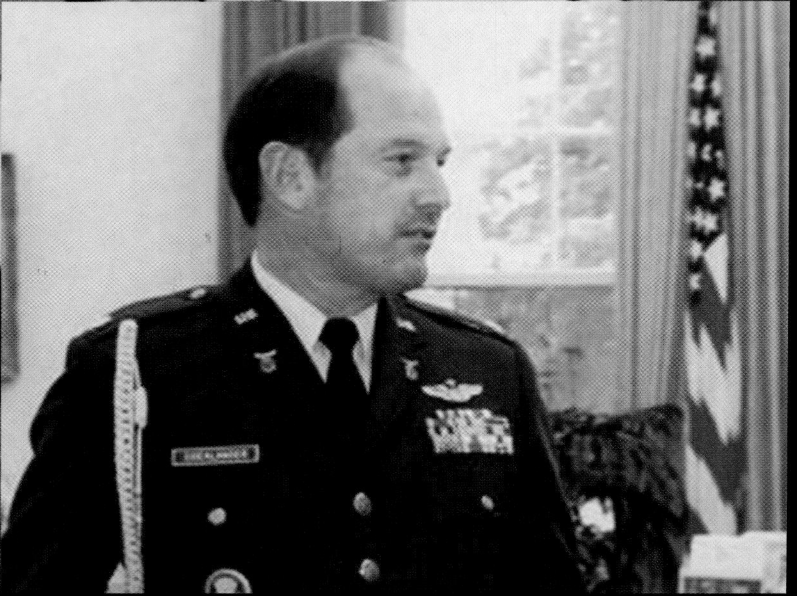

It is difficult to know where to begin when I am asked about my experiences aboard Air Force One. First, I was honored to be onboard this magnificent aircraft, but the true honor was to be onboard in service to President Ronald Reagan as his military aide.

All of the President's travels were significant, but a few had greater historical significance than others, and I was onboard Air Force One for a few of those. We flew to Reykjavik, Iceland, for the second USA-USSR summit with Mikhail Gorbachev full of enthusiasm and then back to the United States full of disappointment.

I was onboard as we flew to Berlin where President Reagan delivered his famous "Mr. Gorbachev, tear down this wall" speech. This trip had added significance for me personally as my father was in Berlin to meet President Reagan on our arrival. My father was meeting the President as part of Berlin's 750th birthday celebration and his contribution to Berlin's history. Dad flew for the United States during the entire Berlin Airlift. The flight from Berlin back to the United States was full of exciting conversations with the President about the "speech" and my father.

One last example of a historical flight aboard Air Force One was in and out of Moscow for the last USA-USSR summit abroad. I can still hear the cheers echoing through the plane when we were wheels-up out of Moscow.

I would again like to say I was proud and honored to have served onboard Air Force One, served President Ronald Reagan, and served the United States of America.

God Bless America.

THE FINAL MISSION

After thousands of hours of effort by hundreds of skilled workers, the day was quickly approaching for the grand opening of Air Force One Pavilion.

It had been over four years since 27000 had touched down at the San Bernardino International Airport after her nonstop flight from Andrews Air Force Base near Washington, D.C. The arrival ceremony and transfer of custody from the United States Air Force to the Ronald Reagan Presidential Library Foundation commenced a process of permanent changes and restoration that would assure the aircraft her appropriate place in history.

The guest list had been drawn, the invitations sent, the media alerted, and the President of the United States had it on his calendar. October 21, 2005, was the date.

Inside the Pavilion, final touches were underway. A genuine Dublin pub named O'Farrell's had been imported directly from Ireland complete with a carved back bar and wooden paneling. It

was brought to the Library in memory of President Reagan, who had visited the pub with Mrs. Reagan in 1984.

A gift shop was installed, featuring merchandise themed on the Pavilion and Air Force One.

An exhibit of the President's travels was established on the mezzanine level. Two flags, Old Glory and the flag of the USSR,

were hung on each side of a slice of the Berlin Wall. When the flags were originally placed, a worker who was a Vietnam veteran alerted the Library staff that the flags were in the wrong position. Sure enough, the Stars and Stripes weren't on the left, as protocol dictated. The staff, under the direction of the Library's curator, Assistant Director John Langellier, quickly made the switch.

Located further along the mezzanine, a room was equipped with displays and a visual presentation on the ending of the Cold War during President Reagan's administration.

The mezzanine leads to the entrance of Air Force One where visitors board through the forward hatch to see the flight deck, the communications center, and the compartment for the President and First Lady, which is complete with a jar of Jelly Belly candies on the desk. The balance of the cabin has areas for staff, crew, and members of the news media. There's even a chocolate cake in the galley for impromptu birthday celebrations.

On October 21, activity and security surrounding the Library was in a heightened state of readiness. Guests parked their personal vehicles in satellite parking locations and were transported by vans to a screening area in front of the Library courtyard. After identifications were confirmed, guests were screened through metal detectors that were staffed by federal government security officers flown in from Washington, D.C.

Once past the entrance processing, guests were allowed to mingle. Most headed for the new Pavilion. The reaction as they entered the long colonnade leading from the main Library to the Air Force One display was universal. There was an air of anticipation and excitement as the nose of Air Force One became visible as soon as they entered the walkway. Once arriving on the overview area of the mezzanine, it was easy to understand why it had earned the nickname "Wow Balcony." There on its three-point perch was Air Force One in all her glory facing Simi Valley through an expansive wall of glass.

A symphony orchestra played on the second level under the plane. Seating was provided under the plane and toward the north wall where a blue stage and background were set up to receive the President and other invited dignitaries.

After several announcements of the program's start, the orchestra struck up a spirited rendition of "Hail to the Chief" and George W. Bush and First Lady Laura Bush made their official entrance accompanied by Nancy Reagan. An all-branch military color guard presented their flags, and the ceremony began.

After several speeches, Mrs. Reagan invited the President and First Lady to see the inside of Air Force One. Afterward, they walked along the elevated mezzanine to the cheers of the large assembly of invited guests. A lunch was served on the lower floor, after which guests visited the displays, had their pictures taken at the entrance of Air Force One, and toured exhibits throughout the Library and Museum.

Photo by Glenn Grossman

The "official" dedication ceremony was followed by two days of invitational events to allow for many others to visit the Pavilion who couldn't attend on Friday.

Media coverage was extensive and very positive. Reviewers agreed that the new Air Force One Pavilion would be a major destination for Southern California residents and visitors from all over the world.

From the moment 27000 touched down in San Bernardino concluding her last flight, a series of accomplishments commenced. Everyone involved said: "Yes, we can!" Each knew he was about to embark on a project that had never before been done.

Photo by Glenn Grossman

Throughout the four-year odyssey, a recurring theme emerged. Witnessing the design and construction of the Air Force One Pavilion and the conscientious disassembly and scrupulous restoration of the legendary aircraft provides tangible assurance that humankind *can* achieve anything and everything it dreams.

Ronald Reagan came from humble beginnings in Illinois that belied his future, much like this Boeing 707. In many ways, the man and the plane have common traits. They both effectively served their country with honor and dignity, often at the same time.

Americans love their heroes. Many who met Ronald Reagan described him as being "larger than life." This assessment could be made of 27000, particularly when viewed inside the Air Force One Pavilion. That the two ended their journeys at the same place is symbolic of the bond that existed between this man and this machine. Each was dependent on the other to rise to their fullest potential; and in the process, they affected the course of history.

Photo by Glenn Grossman

✪ THE FINAL MISSION ✪

Photo by Glenn Grossman

Perhaps it's the optimistic potential of a brighter future that has been encapsulated in the Air Force One Pavilion. The possibilities of tomorrow encourage youth to dream; and through countless examples provided throughout human history, we are granted the belief that our aspirations are limited only by what we can imagine.

Generations of visitors will be the beneficiaries of the vision of a past President who wished to create something special on this hill above Simi Valley. In a most inspiring way, President Reagan and Air Force One are achieving their Final Mission.

INDEX

There were many more photographs of this project but we just didn't have room to include them all in this book. However, we want to take this opportunity to feature just some of the many faces of the tremendous people that worked on bringing Air Force One home.

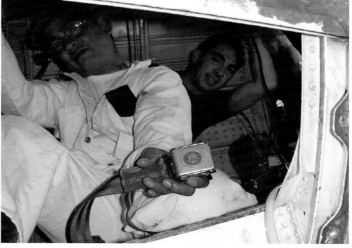

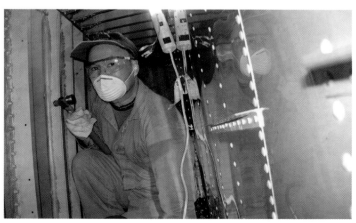

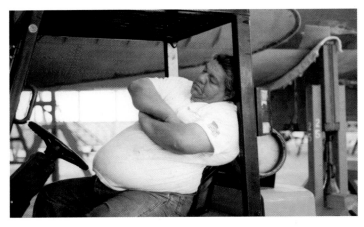

JOEL HASKEL COHEN

When Joel moved his family to Los Angeles in the mid-sixties to pursue his burgeoning acting career, no one, least of all Joel, could have imagined the new direction his life was about to take. A "day job" turned into a full-blown career as one of the industry's top managers, responsible for discovering, developing, and guiding some of the top rock acts and most successful actors in the past thirty years, including Three Dog Night, Cheech & Chong, Steely Dan, David Soul, Carl Weathers, and Willie Aames.

Joel wrote a book about his experiences as Three Dog Night's road manager called *Three Dog Night & Me*, chronicling a tour that started with the band in obscurity and ended with the band in sold-out stadiums as a top-billed act.

When network executives moved to cancel the television series Charles in Charge after the first year, Joel helped launch the plan that would make it the first American sitcom produced exclusively for the TV syndication market. It ran for four more years, and the next phase of his career began.

Joel went to MTV when he heard about a new show called the *MTV Video Music Awards* and convinced the network that he could sell an edited version of the show to markets outside of the United States and Canada. A dozen or so years and numerous concerts and award shows later, Joel was a successful but worn-out producer, writer, and distributor who decided to spend some quality time with his wife, children, and grandchildren and enjoy the fruits of his past labors.

Now, after a little rest and relaxation, his passion to accomplish has been reawakened. Vigorous and determined, he has returned to work.

Photo by Glenn Grossman

MICHAEL STEVEN COHEN

Prior to graduating from the California State University system with a degree in industrial design (product design), Michael Cohen worked for two small design firms and created new products that were successfully marketed by organizations like Xerox Corp., Litton Industries, the United States Navy, Red-E-Kamp, Perma Plaque, Dell Computers, Callen Data Systems, and Aerolog Industries.

Upon graduating, Michael joined Unisys Corporation, then the second largest computer company in the world. He started as a design engineer and, at age twenty-four, managed an eighteen-person design team. After spending six years at Unisys, Michael joined JCP Distribution Inc., an international TV program distribution company as vice president of international sales. He further expanded the distribution business by creating a direct response marketing business for "special interest" videos. Michael formed a partnership with his brother Larry called JCP Video. JCP Video became one of just a few successful direct response companies specializing in video.

Four years after JCP Video was formed, Michael founded Creative Response Inc. and purchased JCP Video as one of its divisions. CRI is a marketing and distribution company that represents a variety of consumer products, including automotive accessories, hardware, sporting goods, electronics, and health and beauty products. Michael travels abroad frequently and has developed relationships with manufacturers worldwide and now services his clients with an active direct import division of CRI.

Michael resides in Southern California with his wife and two children. He has an adventurous spirit and enjoys martial arts, racing cars, traveling, and anything to do with vehicles on land, sea, or air. Michael has over twenty years experience in product design, worldwide sales, and marketing and possesses an ever-present commitment to succeed.

MICHAEL BROGGIE

Michael is a Disney historian and entrepreneur with over 30 years experience developing business relationships. He is co-founder of Broggie & Campbell Productions.

As a nationally recognized public speaker, his many appearances include the UCLA Anderson Graduate School of Management, International Design Conference at Aspen, and the Disney University in Orlando. For the past two years, he appeared as the keynote speaker on the "World's Greatest Hobby" national tour promoting the family hobby of model railroading.

Michael's biography *Walt Disney's Railroad Story* won the Benjamin Franklin Gold Medal in 1998. He wrote the biography of Charles Munger for Peter Kaufman's *Poor Charlie's Almanack* and a child's biography, *Walt Disney's Happy Place*. He has written numerous articles for national magazines.

Michael is married to Sharon Charmagne, an artist and preschool administrator; they reside in Thousand Oaks, California, and are involved in civic and philanthropic activities.